Reading
and Thinking
in English

Discovering
discourse

Teacher's
edition

Reading and Thinking in English

Discovering discourse

Teacher's edition

Oxford University Press
1979

Oxford University Press
Walton Street Oxford OX2 6DP

Oxford London Glasgow New York Toronto
Melbourne Wellington Cape Town Ibadan Nairobi
Dar es Salaam Kuala Lumpur Singapore Jakarta
Hong Kong Tokyo Delhi Bombay Calcutta Madras
Karachi

ISBN 0 19 451356 4

© The British Council 1979

This book is sold subject to the condition that it shall not, by way of trade or otherwise, be lent, re-sold, hired out, or otherwise circulated without the publisher's prior consent in any form of binding or cover other than that in which it is published and without a similar condition including this condition being imposed on the subsequent purchaser.

All rights reserved. No part of this publication may be reproduced, stored in a retrieval system, or transmitted, in any form or by any means, electronic, mechanical, photocopying, recording or otherwise, without the prior permission of Oxford University Press.

Every effort has been made by the publishers to trace the holders of copyright materials used in this book. The publishers would be pleased to hear from any copyright holders who may not have been contacted.

DESIGN BY
Keely + McMahon
ILLUSTRATIONS BY
The Parkway Group
PRINTED IN GREAT BRITAIN AT THE
University Press, Cambridge

Contents

Editor's preface	vii
Preface to the series	viii
Self-study guide	x
Teacher's guide	xiii
Acknowledgements	xxi

Unit 1
Reading as a communicative process

Part 1	Understanding language patterns	3
Part 2	Understanding by the use of context	6
Part 3	Reading with prediction	7
Part 4	Purpose in reading	8
Part 5	Application of the strategies	10

Unit 2
Generalizations

Part 1	The nature of generalizations	15
Part 2	General and specific information (paragraphs containing a single generalization)	16
Part 3	Levels of generality	19
Part 4	Levels of generality expressed by probability, frequency and quantity	23
Part 5	Application of reading strategies to a passage with different levels of generality	28

Unit 3
Descriptions

Part 1	Descriptions and their purposes	33
Part 2	Descriptions of substances and their properties	34
Part 3	Descriptions of processes and their stages	38
Part 4	Ordering information in descriptions	41

CONTENTS

| | Part 5 | Application of reading strategies to a complex description | 46 |

Unit 4
Definitions

	Part 1	The nature of definitions	53
	Part 2	Types of definitions	55
	Part 3	Ways of expressing defining characteristics	59
	Part 4	Expanded definitions	60
	Part 5	Application of reading strategies to a passage concerned with definitions	63

Unit 5
Classifications

	Part 1	The purpose of classifications	70
	Part 2	Types of classifications	72
	Part 3	Ways of expressing classifications	78
	Part 4	Expanded classifications	80
	Part 5	Application of reading strategies to a passage concerned with classifications	83

Unit 6
Hypotheses

	Part 1	The nature of hypotheses	89
	Part 2	Hypotheses and evidence	91
	Part 3	Hypotheses in solving problems	94
	Part 4	Ways of expressing hypotheses	96
	Part 5	Application of reading strategies to a passage concerned with hypotheses	101

Notes on the units — 110

Key — 116

Editor's preface

This course is designed to guide students to the acquisition of strategies of reading in English which they can put to use in following their specialist studies. Although its aim is to provide for specific reading purposes, however, it does not follow the conventional practice of concentrating on how English is used in particular subject areas like Engineering, Economics and so on. Instead a selection is made of topics of more general interest and relevance to learners at this level and these topics are used to demonstrate the communicative functions of English which are common to a whole range of academic writing. The aim, then, is to establish a basic reading competence which can subsequently be brought into more specific focus as it is applied to more specialist uses of English.

Although the emphasis of the course is on how English functions in written communication of a general academic character, the authors recognize that this cannot be adequately dealt with in dissociation from the study of the formal resources of the language. Great care is taken therefore to demonstrate the communicative potential of the grammar itself and to provide practical work which will make the student aware of the functions of grammatical forms in the conveyance of meanings.

The course, then, is integrative in two senses. On the one hand it relates English for Specific Purposes with the teaching of a more general reading competence and on the other hand it shows how the effective teaching of English use must deal with the interdependence of linguistic form and communicative function without concentrating on one at the expense of the other.

H. G. Widdowson
University of London
Institute of Education

Preface to the series

Reading and Thinking in English is an integrated course in reading comprehension for students of English as a foreign language.

A large number of people are learning English not to study the language itself but to study other subjects through English. Reading and Thinking in English is based on the belief that a special kind of course is required for students of English whose main need is to gain access to information through English. The course has been designed for a wide range of learners whose needs can be described as 'English for Academic Purposes'—advanced secondary school pupils preparing for tertiary education, students in universities and other tertiary institutions, adults whose profession requires them to make use of material in English. It is therefore intended to help students and others read textbooks, works of reference and general academic interest, sourcebooks and journals in English.

Sometimes these kinds of learner will consult specialized material in their own field, but they may also be required to read on a wide range of subjects. Consequently, Reading and Thinking in English presents a wide range of writing on topics of general academic interest. It can therefore be used by those following general courses of study as well as more specialist learners. It will also meet some of the needs of Modern Languages students.

The series starts at a near-beginner level. It is assumed that the beginning learner has a minimal knowledge of basic grammar and vocabulary—perhaps he has studied English regularly for a few months, perhaps he has studied it a long time ago or has been learning it irregularly and not very successfully. The course then takes the learner progressively through the intermediate stages of language learning by extending his ability to understand the devices of the language and how they are used in academic communication. By the final book he is expected to have developed a sophisticated awareness of the communicative resources of English and an ability to perform a range of challenging reading tasks.

The series consists of four books. **Concepts in use** extends students' basic knowledge of grammar and vocabulary and how they are used to express fundamental concepts. It also develops their awareness of how passages are built on combinations of these concepts. **Exploring functions** deals with the use of concepts in the communicative function of academic writing. **Discovering discourse** develops students' awareness of how the devices of language are used to express communicative function. It also shows how passages are built on combinations of simple functions. **Discourse in action** extends students' knowledge of the functional organization of written English and develops their ability to handle information found in varied types of real academic discourse. The series is designed so that the books in it can be used independently of the others in the series. Many intermediate or advanced learners may be able to begin with the third or fourth books. The whole series, however, provides a phased approach to the most challenging demands of academic discourse.

Reading and Thinking in English is therefore based on a communicative approach to reading. It assumes that efficient reading requires more than a knowledge of vocabulary and grammatical patterns, and it leads the student to an awareness of how writers structure whole passages and use the grammar and vocabulary of English to communicate. It assumes that reading comprehension can be improved only if students fully understand what they are learning and are prepared to think carefully about how the resources of a language are put to communicative use.

The course was originally developed in the Universidad de los Andes, Bogotá, Colombia, by a project sponsored jointly by the British Council/Ministry of Overseas Development and the Universidad de los Andes. It was initially conceived for

PREFACE TO THE SERIES

university students attending formal classes but has now been extensively revised so that it can also be used for private tuition and self-study. It was tested in classes in several Colombian universities, and when used in formal classes each of the four books is designed to last one semester, so that the whole course provides learning material for a two-year period. It can be used in larger classes as well as with small groups of learners. Students working individually will need to set aside regular study times, although the material lends itself to flexible use. For both formal and informal learning situations the course has been conceived as a realistic route towards efficient and independent study through English.

Self-study guide

This book can be used by students working with a teacher in a class. It can also be used by students working individually and independently. These notes describe the book and suggest how independent students can use it for self-study.

The aim of the book
The aim of the book is to develop efficient comprehension of written academic English (in particular, the English of textbooks). You must be able to understand basic English grammar and vocabulary in order to use the book successfully.

The methods of the book
1   The book develops reading strategies. The strategies are introduced in Unit 1 (Introductory Unit) and practised in all the units. These strategies are the ways an efficient reader extracts information from a passage and uses the information he needs.

2   The book develops an understanding of the methods of organizing information in passages. It is concerned with the *structure* of paragraphs and complete passages, not with the structure of isolated sentences. The structure of a passage depends on the *function* of the passage. For example, some passages have the function of making a definition; others have the function of making a classification. The title of each unit refers to a function of passages. The units practise ways of expressing the functions in English. These functions are common in most academic subjects—Mathematics, Psychology, Engineering, Economics etc.

3   The book develops an understanding of the use of grammar and vocabulary to express the function of passages. For example, Unit 2 studies generalizations. It practises grammar and vocabulary which express probability, frequency and quantity. These areas of grammar and vocabulary are ways of expressing generalizations.

4   The book includes some practice in controlled writing; for example writing summaries or short paragraphs. Many of the comprehension exercises involve writing—usually you can use or adapt sentences from the reading passages. Some students only want to improve their reading. You should do *all* the writing exercises. Writing practice is included because it reinforces reading.

The structure of the book
The book consists of 6 units.
Unit 1   introduces reading strategies
Units 2–5 introduce functions
Unit 6   introduces a new function and provides a complete review of the functions studied in the book.

The structure of the units
Each unit is concerned with a particular function and contains the following elements:

1   Preview. This is a summary of the contents of the unit.

2   An introduction to the nature and purposes of the function. This shows the place of the function in academic communication.

3   Paragraphs which express the function. This shows the structure of paragraphs concerned with the function.

4   Practice in grammar and vocabulary used to express the function.

5   Application of reading strategies to a long passage. Each passage shows how the function is used in a realistic piece of academic English.

Learning activities
The practice activities are all designed to develop reading strategies and the ability to understand how information is organized in passages. They involve answering questions, completing tables and diagrams, making summaries etc. The activities are different because reading involves many different

kinds of tasks. The activities are not mechanical. A reader has to think carefully in order to read with understanding. So reading and thinking are part of the same process.

The method of studying the reading passage in Part 5 of every unit shows some of the aspects of the reading process.

Before the passage there are two types of questions:
1. questions to help you predict the contents of the passage
2. questions to give you a purpose for reading.

On each side of the passage there are language study questions to help you understand the grammar and vocabulary.

After each paragraph there are comprehension questions.

How to use the book
Try to study regularly. It is better to work regularly for a short time than to work occasionally for a long time. It is not a good idea to study more than one part of a unit in one study period. It is a good idea to go back to a previous unit and do a difficult exercise again.

Studying the units
Study the units in the order given in the book.
Study the parts of each unit in the order given.
Study the passages and activities in the order given in the book.
It is dangerous to omit an exercise or change the order of exercises. Many exercises depend on previous ones and follow logically from them.
When you finish Part 5 of each unit, go back to the Preview. Check that you have completed and understood the purpose of each part.

Using the key
After each exercise (or each paragraph of a long reading passage) look at the answers given in the key. Check the answers you gave.

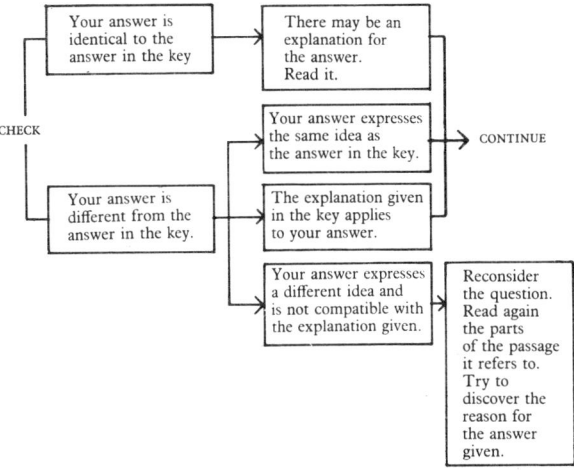

Remember that the answer in the key is not the only correct answer. You may have a different answer and it may be equally acceptable. If you find an exercise particularly difficult, consider very carefully the reasons for the answers in the key. Make a note of the exercise and try it again after a few days.

Use a separate notebook to write your answers to the activities, comprehension and language study questions, and the writing exercises. You will find that most of the comprehension exercises can be done by selecting and writing down the relevant part of the passage. It is not necessary to use your own words: write only what is necessary to answer the questions.

In the summary writing exercises and other writing practice you should write complete sentences. Check the correctness of what you have written before looking at the key.

You will need to use a good dictionary from English into your own language.

When is it necessary to use a dictionary?

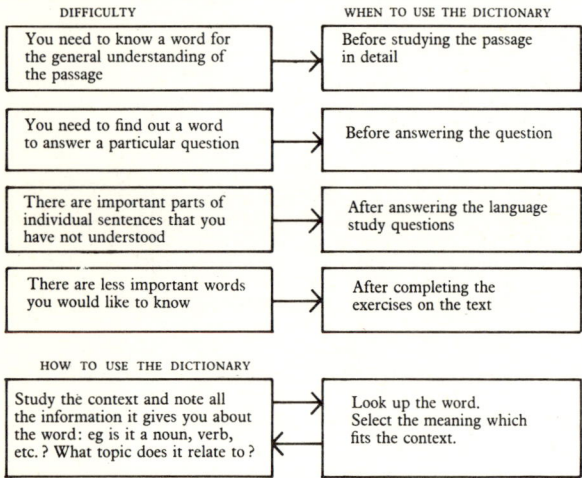

How to use the dictionary
Never read word by word, using the dictionary for everything you do not understand.

If you can, make contact with someone else who is using the book on his own and meet regularly to work with him and discuss your ideas and problems as you go along. The book is not mechanical; each task requires critical thought and is open to discussion.

Teacher's guide

1   Purpose and approach

Discovering discourse considers reading as an integrated process which involves the use of certain reading strategies as well as an understanding of how academic writers communicate in English. The strategies which are introduced are the ways in which an efficient reader extracts information from a passage and then makes use of the information he needs. Throughout the book they are practised separately and combined in the way they contribute to the whole process of reading.

The organization of the book is based on the ways written English is put to communicative use. The essential characteristics of academic communication are not the topics which are written about (such as microscopes, railways, food) but the devices for structuring and presenting information. Academic writing is structured to reflect the kinds of activities that teachers, students or researchers are engaged in—activities such as classifying, defining, describing, explaining, and so on. When we consider how academic writing uses English to communicate information, we can say that the function of a passage or part of a passage is to define, classify, explain, etc. We will therefore refer to these activities as *communicative functions*. These communicative functions are common to many areas of further study. There is therefore no attempt to train students in the English used in any one specific subject area. The authors have found that students can best be prepared to use textbooks in particular subjects by being guided to acquire general strategies for reading and thinking, which they can then transfer to more specialized material.

This guidance is given in **Discovering discourse** by the careful demonstration and controlled exposure to different aspects of written English communication related to topics which are likely to appeal to adult learners, bearing in mind their study purposes.

Both the demonstration and the practice provided in this book are designed to engage the interest and the participation of the students so that they feel that they are really experiencing the language as meaningful communicative behaviour.

2   Design

The book is divided into six units. The first provides an introduction to the strategies which are essential to the communicative process of reading and which are applied to the reading passages at the end of each unit. This first unit, therefore, immediately engages the student's participation and makes him aware of the purpose of the book and of his role in realizing it.

Units 2–6 then deal with certain communicative functions of language which are common in academic writing in general. These are: generalizing, describing, defining, classifying and hypothesizing. The units demonstrate how these functions are realized in English and provide opportunities for the students to apply the reading strategies introduced in Unit 1.

The last unit contains a comprehensive review of the material introduced throughout the book. The design of the book can be represented as:

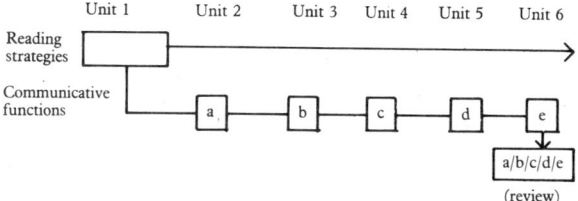

Unit 1 introduces four main reading strategies and then practises applying them to a passage. Units 2–5 each introduce and practise a communicative function and then allow students to apply the reading strategies to a passage which realizes this function. Unit 6 in addition provides an opportunity for relating all the communicative functions introduced in the previous units and so serves as a final review.

The way the different units relate can be shown as follows:

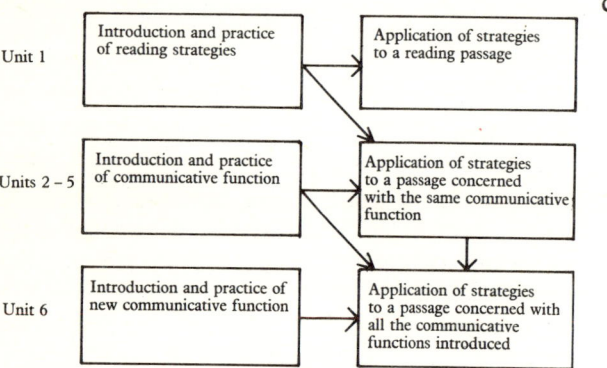

3 Structure of the units

The book is designed to make students aware of how passages are organized to express certain communicative functions. This awareness is developed by organizing the content of each unit so that opportunities are given not only for the practice of reading strategies but also for practice in understanding the use of vocabulary, sentence grammar, and devices which link sentences together to form cohesive units of textual development.

After the first unit has prepared the student for the work of the book, units 2–6 present material in the following way:

a A detailed preview of the contents of the unit. This gives an outline of the unit's contents so that the student is quite clear what is going to be covered.

b An introduction to the communicative nature and purpose of the function focused on in the the particular unit; e.g. the nature and purposes of descriptions, generalizations, definitions etc. This section is designed to exploit what students already know of language and how it works from their experience of using their own mother tongue. In Unit 3, for example, attention is drawn to the different kinds of descriptions to be found in notices, textbooks, advertisements etc. and to the fact that they may be used to inform, warn, persuade and so on.

c Practice in the different realizations of the communicative function concerned. The functions are illustrated by short paragraphs of written English. Unit 2, for example, is concerned with paragraphs expressing a single generalization and paragraphs containing statements of different levels of generality. Unit 3 deals with the use of English for describing substances and processes. Units 4 and 5 introduce the English realizations of different types of definitions and classifications. Unit 6 concentrates on the expression of hypotheses both in relation to evidence and as a basis for deductions. Units 4 and 5 also show how the function dealt with in each unit is expanded by being combined with other functions in a paragraph.

d Practice in understanding areas of vocabulary, points of grammar and cohesive devices in English relevant to the communicative function in focus. Thus Unit 2 is concerned with the use of English for expressing possibility, frequency and quantity, since these are directly relevant to the realization of different levels of generalization. Unit 3 concerns the choice of theme to show new and old information, this being of particular importance in descriptions. Unit 4 deals with the relative clause in English as this device is the main structural means of making definitions. Unit 5 introduces vocabulary related to classifications. Since Unit 6 concentrates on hypotheses it naturally introduces subordinate clauses of conditions and circumstances.

e Practice in applying reading strategies to a longer passage concerned with the function practised in each unit. For example, the passage in Unit 2 shows how a writer makes statements of different levels of generality as part of an explanation of some of the key concepts of ecology. Unit 3 presents a complex type of description—that of a human community. Unit 4 contains a passage in which the precise definition of concepts used in the systems approach is of particular importance. The passage in Unit 5 is concerned with theories of learning and the classification of learning experiments. Unit 6 introduces a substantial report of a piece of research and shows how the various functions studied are integrated into a large scale academic activity.

4   Learning activities

The book introduces a wide variety of learning activities. There are several reasons for this.

1   It seems to the authors that developing reading as a communicative ability can and should involve more than merely reading. Consequently oral and written practice is included. Such activities are designed to increase the students' awareness of the communicative resources of English. This awareness underlies the four skills and thus the practice in other skills helps consolidate the reading ability.

2   The tasks involving reading which students are required to perform as part of their studies are varied and may be expected to include reading and taking notes, writing summaries, planning a project, supplementing lectures and so on. They are required to interpret tables, diagrams, flow charts, graphs etc. all of which put different demands on the reader's abilities. Similarly, students are required to read passages in different ways—sometimes they read to pick out detailed information, sometimes to gain a general impression, and often they must form opinions, use their imagination to catch a writer's implications, criticize and evaluate what they are reading.

3   A variety of activities is seen as an essential pedagogic device to maintain students' interest and show them that each new activity is a new challenge demanding their fullest participation.

It is important, however, that there should be sufficient consistency in practice activities for students to recognize types of practice which are familiar to them. The following are some of the main types of exercises which are found in this book:

– summarizing a passage in the form of a table to show the organization of information in the passage. For example, Activity 3 of Unit 2 leads to the completion of a diagram showing levels of generality:

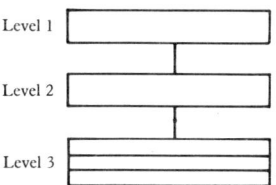

– writing a summary of a reading passage. After each of the long reading passages there is an exercise on summary writing, where students write answers to questions so as to include the main points made in the passage.

– labelling a diagram. For example, in Unit 3 students identify in a diagram some of the components and stages of coffee processing. In order to do this they have to extract the appropriate information from a reading passage.

– reorganizing information and writing statements to express a particular communicative function. For example, in Activity 6 of Unit 4 students are given information in the form of definitions. They then change the way in which the information is presented and rewrite the statements as generaliztions.

There is a particular form of presentation which is used for the long reading passages found in the application stage of each unit, as well as passages in Units 2 and 3. Before each passage there are two types of questions. First, questions for prediction. These questions are designed to make students aware of the importance of predicting what they will find in a passage and to practise ways of doing this. The other type of question is for reading purposes. These questions are designed to allow students to adjust their reading to different types of purposes—such as looking for a factual detail, a main idea, a conclusion or opinion of the writer. On either side of the reading passage itself there is a language study column which focuses students' attention on points of grammar, vocabulary and textual cohesion while they are in the process of reading the passage. After each paragraph of the passage there is a range of comprehension questions. This scheme can be shown as follows:

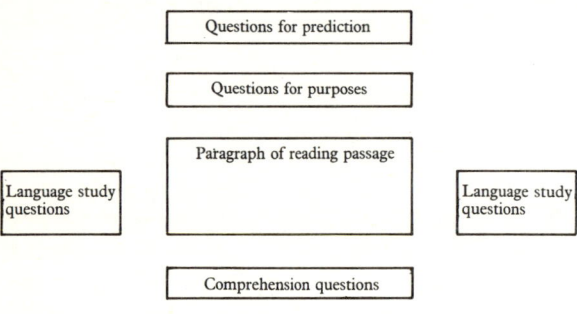

Language study questions
In any paragraph the reader will find one or more numbers. Each number refers to a corresponding language study question. The reader therefore knows what part of the passage each language study question refers to.

The language study questions are of three types:
1 Questions to practise contextual deductions (deducing the meaning of an unfamiliar word by using knowledge of the context which surrounds that word). Some of these questions draw attention to the part of the context which will help and to the kind of deductions which can be made. Others give alternative equivalents (such as might be found in a monolingual dictionary) and require students to choose the closest equivalent. It is important to remember that these questions, although concerned with individual vocabulary items, are designed not to test understanding of a particular word but to develop students' strategies of deduction.
2 Questions to practise understanding difficult sentence structures.
3 Questions to practise understanding relations between sentences.

Comprehension questions
Two main kinds of comprehension skills are developed. These are:
– the ability to make relationships between pieces of information and ideas given in different parts of a passage and to reorganize them according to a particular purpose. Sometimes the student has to make a list of points mentioned or reorganize the information in a particular way.
– the ability to understand a writer's inferences and implications and seeing the relative importance that the writer gives to different pieces of information.

5 How to use the book—some general considerations
There are a certain number of questions that teachers often ask when confronted with a course in reading comprehension. Some of these are answered below.

Q Should the teacher concentrate 100% on reading or should he give some practice in oral and writing skills?

A The authors certainly recommend controlled writing practice (this is stimulated regularly in the book), and some oral participation. However, both speaking and writing should be seen as contributing to more efficient reading and should not be allowed to dominate the course. The amount of importance given to these skills will vary according to the aims of the course. However, it is particularly important when testing students that their accuracy in writing should not count for more than, say, 10% of the total mark.

Q Should the teacher prohibit the use of the native language, translation and the use of a bilingual dictionary?

A Certainly not. The teacher may wish to use the native language to explain a teaching point or unfamiliar words, or to clarify an exercise or any parts of the study procedure. It may be preferable for students to answer some questions in the native language if the answer they wish to give cannot be extracted from a reading passage. It may also be preferable for them to discuss or justify their answers in their own language. It should, however, be remembered that exercises which use production as a way of consolidating particular language patterns should be done only in English. We do not recommend that complete passages should be translated, but the teacher may wish to translate a sentence or part of a sentence or ask students to do so. The teacher is advised to use translation as one way of showing comprehension and not as a way of improving it. The use of a bilingual dictionary is recommended and it is suggested not only that the teacher should where possible require students to use one, but also that he should help them to use it effectively. Contextual deduction, for example, may sometimes replace looking a word up in a dictionary, but it remains necessary even when a bilingual dictionary is used.

Q What about grammar?
A This book is for students who have at least a passive understanding of basic grammar. Grammar points which are relevant to the communicative function being studied are introduced in most units. The teacher's notes to each unit suggest how further grammar practice can be given if desired. At this stage, however, it is not considered that much practice of grammar patterns in isolation is necessary. If the learning of grammar is to contribute to reading efficiency, it must be concentrated on the meanings that grammatical devices are used to express.

Q Should teaching points be explained?
A It is important that the teacher should help students understand what they are doing and why they are doing it. It is therefore essential to clarify and emphasize the main points in each part of the units. The teacher should encourage students to think about the functions studied and how they are realized. However, the teacher should resist the temptation to turn classes into a talk about the communicative functions being studied. The book aims to show students how these functions are realized in academic English, so it is not necessary for the teacher to explain at length the logic of definition, for example. Nor is it necessary to require students to say what the difference is between a real and a nominal definition. The communicative functions are being taught as an aid to comprehension, not as ends in themselves, so it is better to test students on the final aim of comprehension than on their mastery of all the means of getting there.

Q What is the role of the teacher?
A The coursebook itself contains the minimum path through the course—it has enough reading passages to illustrate the teaching points and a full sequence of exercises for each. It is not therefore necessary for the teacher to supplement it with extra material, or for him to devise extra teaching exercises unless he so wishes. The teacher's role, which remains very important, includes:
– motivating students towards the topics of the readings and the teaching points of each unit. On the one hand the teacher can start with an aspect of the topic which is familiar to students and arouse their curiosity to read further. On the other hand the teacher may explore what students already know of the function being studied.
– providing clarification, explanation and

occasional translation of teaching points or study activities
- planning the overall distribution of time and managing the classroom activities (see next section)
- guiding students having particular difficulties
- ensuring full student participation, checking work and evaluating the acceptability of answers. The latter is particularly important as most questions can be answered in different ways and it is suggested that the teacher should regularly ask students to justify answers and be the final arbiter of the appropriacy of their contributions.
- keeping a record of students' progress, designing and administering tests.

6 How to use the book—classroom management

The authors' main recommendation is that classroom time is divided equally in three ways: having the students work as a class (listening either to the teacher or to a fellow student), in groups, and individually. Having the students work as a class is most appropriate for introducing a new stage of the unit, discussing answers and drawing conclusions. Group work is preferable wherever students can profit by discussing their ideas with their fellows and will probably be found appropriate for many of the activities in the book. Individual work is most suited to the more controlled type of exercise (particularly writing) where there is less to discuss and it is important that all students should produce a response.

The three types of work can be alternated so as to ensure variety, as is illustrated by the following suggestions:

I = individual
G = group
C = class
S = students
T = teacher

Unit 4	Definitions
I	Preview S read silently.
Part 1	
I-C	T introduces. S study passage and prepare answers to questions 1–7. T asks for oral answers and checks.
C	T goes up to Activity 1 reading aloud and asking individual students.
I-C	Activity 1 is done individually and checked in class.
Part 2	
G-C	Activity 2 The passage is read and discussed and answers are worked out in groups. Answers are checked and explanation is covered in class.
I	Activity 3
C-I-C	Activity 4 Explanation is covered in class, and exercise is written individually and checked in class.
Part 3	
I-C	Activity 5
C-I-C	Activity 6 T does one further example with students and makes sure that procedure for the exercise is understood. Answers are then written individually and checked in class.
Part 4	
G-C	Activity 7
I-C	Activity 8 (there is probably less to be discussed here than in activities 7 and 9).
G-C	Activity 9
Part 5	
C	Go up to the end of the three questions for prediction.
I-C	Reading for purpose is done individually and checked in class.
I-G-C	Comprehension questions are discussed and answered in groups after individuals

TEACHER'S GUIDE

	have read the relevant paragraph. Answers are then discussed in class.
I-C	Language study questions.
I-C	Summary writing.

Because much of the book is suitable for individual work, students can be set regular assignments out of class. These can take one of two forms:

a preparing material (such as a reading passage) for subsequent discussion in class.

b writing up exercises introduced in class. For instance: an example of an exercise is written up on the board, two more answers are given orally. The teacher is then satisfied that the class knows how to tackle it and sets the whole exercise as a writing assignment.

It is suggested that the teacher should require all written work (including the completion of diagrams, answers to questions, summaries etc.) to be done in a separate notebook.

F. Smith	*Comprehension and Learning*	HOLT RINEHART
D. Wilkins	*Notional Syllabuses*	OUP
M. Coulthard	*Introduction to Discourse Analysis*	LONGMAN
H. Widdowson	*Teaching Language as Communication*	OUP
Halliday & Hasan	*Cohesion in English*	LONGMAN
Open University Reading Development Course	*The Reading Process*	OPEN UNIVERSITY

Distribution of time

The teacher will have to deal with this extremely flexibly, so the following should only be considered as suitable for some circumstances but not for all. The course has been designed to last approximately 60 class periods of 50 minutes plus about 20 out-of-class assignments. This means that the units can be expected to last an average of 10 class periods. Units 3 and 6 may require slightly more than this but the teacher should try and avoid allowing particular units to dominate the others.

Background reading

This book is based on a communicative approach to reading and language teaching. The teacher will find useful background reading on these two aspects in the following books:

Leech & Svartvik	*A Communicative Grammar of English*	LONGMAN

xix

Acknowledgements

Reading and Thinking in English was initially developed in a project sponsored jointly by the University of the Andes, Bogotá, Colombia, and the British Overseas Development Ministry in association with the British Council.

The Director of the project was John Moore, of the British Council, and the members of the University who participated in the writing of **Discovering Discourse** were Luisa Fernanda de Knight, Teresa Munévar M, and Dora Bonnet de Salgado.

The materials have been revised and extended by John Moore and Teresa Munévar in the Department of English as a Foreign Language of the University of London Institute of Education under the guidance of the Associate Editor, Professor H. G. Widdowson.

The publishers would like to thank the following people and organizations for their assistance and co-operation in developing Reading and Thinking in English for publication:

    The University of the Andes, Bogotá.

    The British Council in London and Bogotá.

    The University of London Institute of Education.

The publishers would like to thank the following for permission to base a number of illustrations on original drawings from the following sources:

Collier's Encyclopedia, © 1963. Adapted as figure, page 43 by permission of *Crowell-Collier Publishing Company*.
Anne Harris, **Man's Environment**, © 1972. Adapted as figure, page 44 by permission of *Macdonald Educational Ltd*.
Henry Jacabowitz, **Electronics Made Simple**, © 1977. Adapted as figure, page 46 by permission of *W. H. Allen & Co. Ltd*.
Samuel W. Matthews, **This Changing Earth**, © 1973. Figures, page 92 based on National Geographic map and diagrams by permission of *National Geographic Magazine*.
Nelson & Geselowitz, **The Theoretical Basis of Electrocardiology**, © 1976. Adapted as figure, page 64 by permission of *The Clarendon Press, Oxford*.
Oxford Junior Encyclopedia 3, Edited by Jean K. F. Petrie, © 1973. Adapted as figures, pages 35, 64, 98, 137 by permission of *Oxford University Press*.
Magnus Pyke, **Man and Food**, © 1970. Adapted as figure, page 53 by permission of *Weidenfeld & Nicholson Ltd*.
A. F. Wells, **Structural Inorganic Chemistry**, 4th Ed., © 1975. Adapted as figures, page 35 by permission of *The Clarendon Press, Oxford*.
Edmond Capon, **Princess of Jade**, ©. Photograph by William MacQuitty adapted as figure, page 33 by permission of *Thomas Nelson & Sons Ltd*.

Although every effort has been made to trace copyright holders, this has proved impossible in some cases. If any copyright holders incorrectly acknowledged will contact the publisher, corrections will be made in future editions.

The publishers would like to thank the following for permission to reproduce their work:

photograph, page 3: John T. Lindquist II;
cartoon, page 12: Paddy Mounter.

Early versions of materials for this book and other titles in the series were used in trial teaching by the following Colombian universities:

    Universidad Nacional, Bogotá.
    Universidad Social Católica de la Salle, Bogotá.
    Universidad Pedagógica y Tecnológica de Colombia, Tunja.
    Universidad del Norte, Barranquilla.
    Universidad del Valle, Cali.

Unit 1 Reading as a communicative process

Preview

This unit presents some strategies to help improve reading efficiency.

The unit is in five parts. Each part deals with a particular reading strategy, as follows:

Part 1
provides practice in understanding language patterns.

Part 2
provides practice in understanding by the use of context.

Part 3
develops the ability to read with prediction.

Part 4
is concerned with purpose in reading.

Part 5
applies the reading strategies that were developed in parts 1–4 to the study of an unsimplified passage.

These strategies will be practised throughout the the book. This unit therefore introduces the method of working which will be used in all of the other units.

Part 1
Understanding language patterns

There are different ways of communicating:

by means of visual images,

by means of actions and gestures,

by means of language.

The same message can be conveyed by different means:

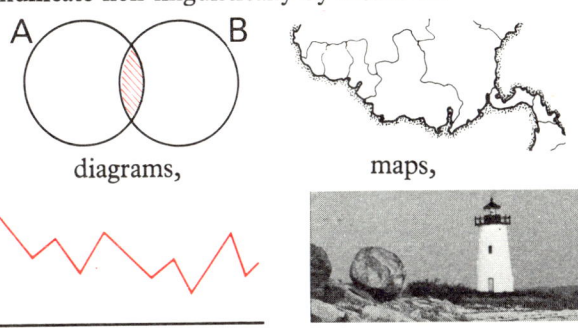

visually   and linguistically.

Books communicate linguistically. They also communicate non-linguistically by means of:

diagrams,   maps,

graphs,   pictures.

In order to understand a visual form of communication you must understand visual symbols.

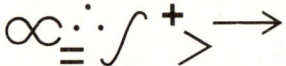

Writing also uses visual symbols:

In order to convey a message, visual symbols have to be grouped into patterns:

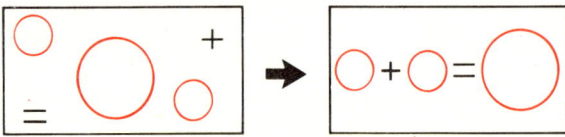

Similarly, linguistic symbols are grouped into patterns:

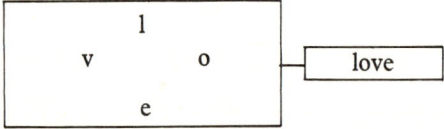

The same units can be grouped into different patterns:

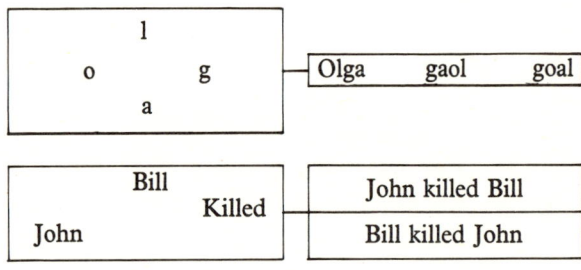

Some patterns make no sense:

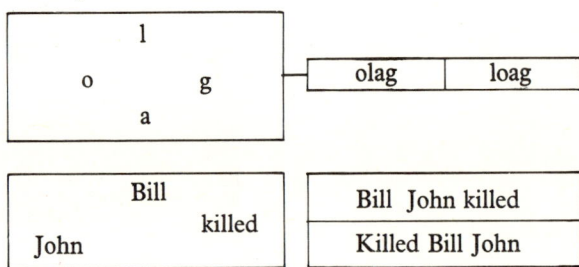

Part 1 UNDERSTANDING LANGUAGE PATTERNS

Reading requires a knowledge of how linguistic symbols combine to make words and sentences in English, and of what these words and sentences mean.

Activity 1

Understanding the meanings of word and sentence patterns

Below is a description of a spaceship by somebody who said he had seen it—an eyewitness. With it there is a drawing of the spaceship. Read the eyewitness's account and write down the sections of it that do not correspond to the drawing. Then rewrite those sections so that they do correspond. Notice what changes in grammar and vocabulary you make in your corrections.

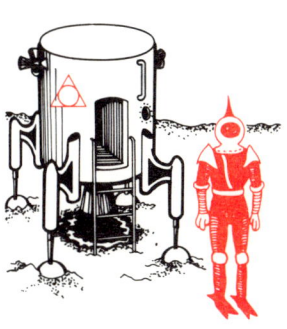

The spaceship was about two metres high. It was round at the bottom and pointed at the top. The craft was supported by three legs which were taller than the main body of the ship. I saw a small green man with two horns who had probably jumped from the ship as there was no ladder. I remember clearly a mysterious sign on the side of the craft. It showed a triangle surrounded by a circle. I am sure this is a message to people on Earth.

Activity 2

Reading, however, does not stop at understanding word and sentence patterns. Sentences are arranged into larger patterns in order to present information in a logical way. It is possible to understand every word in a passage without understanding the message. What is wrong with the following passage?

It is well known that cats are more intelligent than dogs. For example, three out of every four motorists die of heart disease before they are fifty. Another example is the commonly observed ability of dolphins to understand human speech.[1] In conclusion I should like to emphasize that whereas girls learn mathematics quickly, boys learn mathematics equally quickly.[2]

[2] Does the final sentence contain two contrasting ideas?

[1] Do the examples support the generalization?

Unit 1 READING AS A COMMUNICATIVE PROCESS

The logical structure of a passage depends on how the writer wants to present the information in it. The logical structure of a passage is often signalled by expressions which connect ideas together. These are called textual connectors. They act as signposts to help you find your way through the passage. Underline the expressions in the above passage which have this function.

We can now summarize the first strategy for improving reading. Recognize patterns of language inside the sentence and between sentences by increasing your understanding of vocabulary, grammar and textual connectors.

Part 2 Understanding by the use of context

There are many occasions when you meet words or phrases which you do not know. A different set of strategies is needed for solving problems caused by unfamiliar words or phrases in a passage. One of these strategies is to deduce the meaning of these words or phrases by referring to the words and phrases that you do know. For example, you may find an unfamiliar word in this sentence:

The Noanamá Indians cut their canoes out of tree trunks by using an adze.

Try and draw an adze using information in the sentence. Try to complete the following statements.

An adze is a kind of .... It can be used for .... ∴ (therefore) it is similar to a ....

Activity 3

Below is a paragraph followed by a list of words from it. Try and deduce the meaning of the words in the list by reference to the grammar and connectors in the sentences in the paragraph. In each case consider which words in the context helped you, and how they helped you.

Some photographic operations, such as masking and dodging, can easily be done by the amateur. Control of the contrast of different parts of the negative is achieved by dodging. One type of dodging is known as burning in. Burning in, the darkening of light areas, is done by using a hole in a piece of cardboard. Some parts of the negative may have to be 'held back' because they are too dark. The photographer can also decide how much of the negative to print. He may decide to print the complete negative, or, on the other hand, he may crop it.

LIST OF WORDS
dodge   burn in
hold back crop

There is a relation between the helpful part of the context and each word from the list. Which of the following relations helped you deduce the meaning of each word?

a   contrast
b   cause/consequence
c   general/specific
d   method/purpose
e   equivalence

We can now summarize the second strategy for improving reading. Use the information from the context to discover the meaning of unfamiliar words or phrases and to help choose the appropriate meaning from the dictionary.

**Part 3
Reading
with prediction**

The two strategies described above will help you read more accurately and fluently. There is another technique that will help you read more fluently. This strategy is to *predict* as much as you can about what you are reading. The title of a book, article or passage tells you the topic of what you will read. Use your own knowledge of the topic to predict as much as you can about the contents.

Activity 4

Here are some titles. What information would you expect to find in passages with these titles?

Unit 1 READING AS A COMMUNICATIVE PROCESS

1	Sports and international relations
2	Why it is necessary to stop drug addiction
3	Chess for beginners

Activity 5

Non-linguistic devices, like those shown on page 3, can also provide a context for prediction. What would you expect to find in the text accompanying this picture?

The Water Cycle   Names of things   Actions

Activity 6

Use your knowledge of the context to make predictions. Here are the beginnings of some passages. How would you expect them to continue?

1   There are several reasons for the collapse of the bridge ......
2   The consumption of alcoholic drinks in Europe is increasing. For example, ...
3   If we compare the salaries of men and women engineers in the United States we find that men earn more at the top of the profession whereas......
4   Two of the most interesting aspects of termites are their methods of obtaining food and their social organization. With respect to their feeding habits there have been remarkable observations of how they cultivate fungus. As for the second aspect......

We can now summarize the third strategy.
Make predictions about the content of a passage based on:
1   title, subtitles and your own knowledge of the topic
2   non-linguistic context: pictures, diagrams etc.
3   the linguistic context.

Part 4
Purpose in reading

There is a final set of strategies which will help you read more efficiently. We saw in Activity 2 in Part 1

Part 4   PURPOSE IN READING

that writers structure the information in a passage according to the purpose they have in mind. In the same way a reader has a purpose. In order to read efficiently you must be able to find in a passage the information which is necessary for your purpose. This means you can often ignore what is not relevant for your purpose.

Activity 7   Let us consider the kinds of purposes people have when reading. Look at the following pieces of information and suggest a purpose for reading each one.

1

Smith, Henry J.   15 Brookville Avenue
　　　Birmingham 15　　　　　　　　　　994 7162
Smith, Henry K.   20 Park Street
　　　Birmingham 12　　　　　　　　　　931 8429

2

Attractive woman, 35, interested in music and horses. Wishes to meet gentleman of similar age and interests.

3

Cut the onions into small pieces and fry gently.

4

FOR SALE
Gruntone tape recorder! Second-hand.
Good working order.

Activity 8   Two people may read the same passage in different ways because their purposes are different. A common purpose in reading is to find some information.

1   Choose one item from the following list and read the passage about bridges to obtain the relevant information.

INFORMATION REQUIRED
a　Different forms of bridges.
b　Materials bridges are made of.
c　The construction date of the Sydney Harbour Bridge.

9

Unit 1 READING AS A COMMUNICATIVE PROCESS

    d   The longest suspension bridge.
    e   The difference between modern and primitive bridges.
    f   The circumstances appropriate for building a suspension bridge.

BRIDGES
Until recent times the commonest form of bridge was the arch, usually made of stone, brick or wood. The introduction of iron and steel during the Industrial Revolution changed bridge design completely. There is now a wide variety of forms for different purposes. The suspension bridge has often been chosen for long spans. Examples of these are the Sydney Harbour Bridge (1932, 650 m), the Forth Road Bridge (1961, 1100 m), and the Golden Gate (1400 m). Reinforced concrete is now in common use for bridges carrying roads.

2   Now underline the parts of the passage which were relevant for your purpose.
3   Which of the following did your reading involve?
    a   Finding one specific piece of information.
    b   Making a list of specific pieces of information.
    c   Making a deduction from different pieces of information.

We can now summarize the fourth strategy for improving reading. **Have a clear purpose before reading; locate the parts of a passage which are relevant to your purpose.**

Activity 9

Using the summaries given at the end of each part, write a summary of this unit under the title *Strategies for Reading*.

**Part 5
Application of the strategies**

We can now use the strategies studied in Parts 1–4 to read a passage.

Part 5 APPLICATION OF THE STRATEGIES

1   USING THE TOPIC TO READ WITH PREDICTION (see Part 3)

The title of the passage is 'Are we afraid to be different?' It describes an experiment which investigates whether people can be made to agree with others. Which of the following pieces of information would you expect to find in the passage?

The purpose of the experiment.
The number of participants.
The task they were required to do.
The colour of the participants' hair.
The result of the experiment.
A description of the town in which it took place.
The kind of pressure that was used.

2   READING WITH PURPOSE (see Part 4)

Now read the whole passage rapidly in order to find out whether the information you selected from the list above is given. Concentrate on the parts of the passage that are relevant for this purpose. Do not use the dictionary yet, and do not answer the language study and comprehension questions.

Next, read the whole passage again in the same way to find the answers to the following questions. Mark the sections of the passage which give you the answers.

a   Does the writer say the people are easily made to conform?
b   What does the writer think of the results of the experiment?

3   UNDERSTANDING LANGUAGE PATTERNS AND THE USE OF CONTEXT (see Parts 1 and 2)

Read the first paragraph carefully in order to answer the comprehension questions after it. If you have difficulty in understanding the paragraph the language study questions in the margins may help you. However, you do not need to answer all the language study questions now. Study the second paragraph in the same way.

Unit 1 READING AS A COMMUNICATIVE PROCESS

ARE WE AFRAID TO BE DIFFERENT?

It is well known that when an individual joins a group he tends to accept the group's standards of behaviour and thinking. He is expected to behave in accordance with these norms[1]— in other words the group expects him to conform.[2] Many illustrations could be given of this[3] from everyday life, but what is of particular interest to psychologists is the extent to which people's judgements and opinions can be changed as a result of group pressure.[4] Some remarkable conclusions were reported by Asch and others (1952). They noticed that people in a group will agree to statements that are contrary to the evidence of their senses or that contradict their own beliefs. It would be a mistake to think that only particularly docile people are chosen to take part in experiments of this type. Usually highly intelligent and independent[5] people are used and this, of course, makes the results even more disturbing.

1 What have the experiments demonstrated?
2 Why are the results disturbing?

In a typical experiment, this is what may happen. The experimenter asks for volunteers to join a group which is investigating visual perception. The victims are not, therefore, aware of the real purpose of the experiment.[6] Each volunteer is taken to a room where he finds a group of about seven people who are collaborating with the experimenter. The group is shown a standard card which contains a single line. They are then asked to look at a second card. This has three lines on it. One is obviously longer than the line on the first card, one is shorter and one the same length. They have to say which line on the second card is the same length as the line on the standard card. The other members of the group answer first but what the volunteer does not know is that they have been told to pick one of the wrong lines.[7] The volunteer sees that the other members of the group unanimously choose a line which is obviously not the same length as the one on the standard card.

Side notes

[1] The individual is expected to behave according to the ...... of the group.

[2] The expression *in other words* indicates that the statements it connects mean the same ∴ *conform* means ....

[3] *this* refers to a fact already mentioned. What fact does it refer to?

[4] What are psychologists particularly interested in?

[5] Which of the following can be deduced from this context?
a *docile* means the same as *independent*
b *docile* means the opposite of *independent*
∴ *docile people* in this context means people who
 i are easily influenced
 ii are difficult to influence
 iii co-operate with other people in groups

[6] Do the volunteers know the real purpose of the experiment?

[7] Who have been told to pick the wrong line?

When it is his turn to answer he is faced with the unanimous opinion of the rest of the group—all the others have chosen line A but he quite clearly sees line B as correct.[8] What will he do? According to Asch, more than half of the victims chosen will change their opinion. What is equally surprising[9] is that, when interviewed about their answers, most explained that they knew the group choice was incorrect but that they yielded to the pressure of the group because they thought they must be suffering from an optical illusion, or because they were afraid of being different.[10] However, Asch also found that if he allowed one correct judgement in the group the probability of the victim conforming was dramatically decreased. Perhaps this is the most encouraging finding in real-life terms:[11] if we have the courage to keep to our beliefs, we may give others the courage to express theirs.

[8] All the other members of the group state the same opinion. They are unanimous.
∴ a *unanimous* opinion is one which is shared by ....

[9] What two facts are surprising?

[10] What was the effect of the pressure? ∴ *yield* to pressure means *oppose/not oppose* pressure.

[11] Which is the most encouraging finding?

3   Using the description in the paragraph, draw the lines which were on each card.
4   In what circumstances do most people yield to pressure? In which do few people yield to pressure?
5   What explanations are given for:
    a   the wrong choice of the victims
    b   the wrong choice of the other members of the group?

Now go back and answer any language study questions that you did not answer earlier.

Unit 2 Generalizations

Preview
This unit develops the ability to distinguish different levels of generality in a passage. It draws attention to the importance of using information from the context in order to distinguish the different levels.

Part 1
draws attention to the nature of generalizations.

Part 2
deals with general and specific information in paragraphs containing a single generalization.

Part 3
introduces the concept of levels of generality through paragraphs containing statements with different levels of generality.

Part 4
deals with the use of expressions of likelihood, quantity and frequency to indicate different levels of generality.

Part 5
applies the reading strategies that were developed in Unit 1 to a passage which contains statements of different levels of generality.

Part 1
The nature of generalizations

Activity 1

This activity illustrates the difference between general and specific statements.

The following statements appeared in a survey of the use made by students of libraries over one academic year.

a   Most psychology students do not use libraries.
b   In the months of February and March, only 14% of Psychology students used the University library.
c   In the months of February and March, 20% of the students used the University library.
d   Most psychology students do not use the University library.
e   The majority of students do not use libraries.

Now answer these questions about the five statements above.

1   Which statements do not refer to a specific period of time?
2   Which statements do not refer to specific groups of students?
3   Which statements do not refer to a specific library?
4   Which statement is most specific?
5   Which statement is most general?

We can distinguish specific statements which are true for specific quantities, times, events, etc. from more general statements which attempt to cover a wider range of events and times. When we read passages we often find specific and general statements together. So it is important to be able to distinguish the more general statements from the more specific. We must also consider how the specific statements support and justify the generalizations.

Unit 2 GENERALIZATIONS

**Part 2
General and specific information**

We will now study paragraphs which contain a generalization and more specific information. Here is the first paragraph of a passage on Transport Functions. Read through the paragraph once in order to find the generalization. Underline the generalization.

Planning of transport organization should consider the functions of transport in society. One obvious function is the movement of people for work and leisure. Transportation, however, is equally concerned with the movement of goods.[1] Goods have little value unless they are in the right place at the right time.

1   What examples of transport functions are mentioned?
2   What is the important thing about transporting goods?
3   Complete the following table to show the relationship between the generalization and the specific information.

[1] From the context, deduce the meaning of the word *goods*. Does it mean:
a   one of the purposes (such as work or leisure) of moving people
b   certain kinds of people who need to use transport
c   something other than people that can be transported?

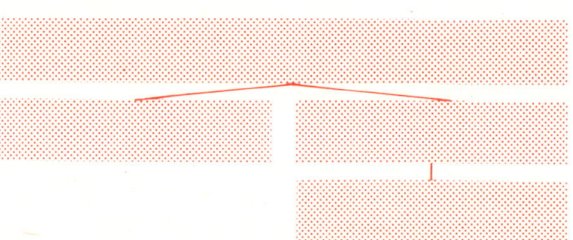

Generalization

Examples of functions

Example which justifies the generalization

The answers to the comprehension questions show the relation between specific information and the generalization. Now answer the language study question.

READING WITH PREDICTION
Now that you have read the first paragraph, which of the following aspects would you expect to find in the rest of the passage?

The reasons why goods need to be transported.
The date of the invention of the hovercraft.
The importance of avoiding transport delays.

Part 2 GENERAL AND SPECIFIC INFORMATION

The way in which industry relies on transport.
The leisure opportunities in present-day society.

PURPOSE IN READING
Read the rest of the passage rapidly in order to find out which of the above aspects are included in the passage.

UNDERSTANDING LANGUAGE PATTERNS
Now read each paragraph carefully in order to answer the comprehension questions on general and specific information. If you have difficulty in understanding the paragraphs, the language study questions in the margins may help you. However, you do not need to answer all the language study questions now.

³
What is done to iron ore in the plants?

⁴
Ore contains metal and waste. We do not want to transport the waste.
∴ the ores are reduced.
So *reduce* means separate the . . . . . . from the metal in an . . . .

Raw materials are seldom consumed where they occur in nature. Coal and iron ore, materials essential to steel and iron production,[2] must be transported from their widely-located natural deposits to specific melting plants.[3] Copper and some other non-ferrous ores are often reduced at the mines to avoid the transport of large quantities of waste materials,[4] whereas timber has its full value in consumer areas.[5] Much of Sweden's timber, Malaya's rubber, the U.S.'s grain, Kuwait's oil, New Zealand's meat and Australia's wool requires international transport in order to be of value.

²
What materials mentioned are essential to steel and iron production?

⁵
Are timber and copper said to be alike or unlike? In what way?

4   List the materials which:
    a   are partially consumed where they occur
    b   are not consumed where they occur.
5   Is it common for raw materials to be consumed where they occur? ∴ in this context does *seldom* mean *commonly* or *not commonly*?
6   Underline the generalization in the paragraph.
7   Use information in the paragraph to write an example of this generalization. Include:
    a   a specific raw material
    b   why it has to be transported.

Unit 2   GENERALIZATIONS

Equally obvious is the importance of time for the transport of many goods.⁶ Fresh fruits, vegetables and fish, even when refrigerated, are vulnerable to delays in transit. If car component deliveries are held up for only a few days, massive cost increases result from disturbance of the production lines.⁷ Newspapers and mail are even more susceptible to delay.⁸ So transport and communication retain a vital relationship despite the telephone, radio and television.

8   Underline the generalization in the paragraph.
9   Use information in the paragraph to write an example of this generalization. Include:
   a   specific goods
   b   why time is important for their transportation.
10   List the forms of communication mentioned which depend on rapid transport, and those which do not.
11   Complete: *Delays to car component deliveries cause* ...... *This causes* ......

Consider the ways in which an industrial manufacturing concern may be involved in transport. Coal and oil must be moved to the electricity generating station which satisfies the manufacturer's power requirements. Raw materials must be carried to the production units. Components (some of which must be imported) must be moved at a regular rate to the assembly plant.⁹ The distribution and exporting of completed products requires other types of transportation services. Transport costs are therefore a vital element in industrial productivity.¹⁰

Adapted from: J. K. Canell. *Transport* in *The Man Made World*, Open University Technology Foundation Course

12   Underline the generalization in the paragraph.
13   Use information in the paragraph to write an example of this generalization. Include:
   a   what has to be transported

⁶ Find the sentence in paragraph 1 that indicates the two things that are equally obvious.

⁷ Fresh fruits are affected by delays. The car industry is also affected by delays to car component deliveries. Underline the words in the paragraph which mean *delayed*.

⁸ Fresh fish is vulnerable to delay. Newspapers are also vulnerable to delay. Underline the word in the paragraph which means *vulnerable*.

⁹ What must be imported?

¹⁰ Does this paragraph indicate that the place of transport costs in industry is:
   a   not important
   b   increasing
   c   extremely important
   d   of small importance?
∴ *vital* means ......

Part 3   LEVELS OF GENERALITY

    b   where it has to be taken
    c   for what purpose it is required.

14   Which example in this paragraph refers to time?

15   Complete the diagram to summarize the final paragraph. Use items from the list on the right.

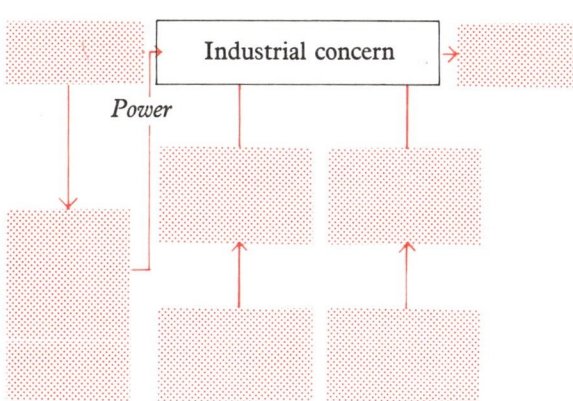

raw materials
coal and oil
components
assembly plant
completed products
electricity generating
   station
production units

Now answer any language study questions that you did not answer earlier.

WRITING A SUMMARY
Finally, write a summary of the whole passage using the generalizations you found in each paragraph.

Part 3
Levels of generality

In Part 1 you studied paragraphs containing a single generalization. In this part you will study paragraphs containing generalizations of different levels.

Activity 2

Study the following groups of sentences. In each group one sentence is a generalization and the other three are examples which support it. Write down the generalization from each group.

GROUP 1
The mass media are often badly used.
Newspapers only give sensational news.
Radio programmes are usually superficial.
Television has bad effects on people.

Unit 2 GENERALIZATIONS

GROUP 2
Television commercials distort the truth about products.
Crime films on television encourage violence.
Television has bad effects on people.
Television documentaries stop people from thinking independently.

GROUP 3
Toothpaste does not make teeth white.
Television commercials distort the truth about products.
The safety of electrical goods is exaggerated.
Many widely-advertised pain-killers are not effective.

Notice that the generalization from Group 2 can serve as an example from Group 1. Similarly, the generalization in Group 3 illustrates the generalization in Group 2. We can therefore conclude that the three generalizations have different levels of generality.

Notice also that the sentence *Television has bad effects on people* is an example in Group 1 and a generalization in Group 2. Similarly, the sentence *Television commercials distort the truth about products* is an example in Group 2 and a generalization in Group 3. We can therefore conclude that the level of generality depends on the context.

Activity 3

1   Here is a list with different levels of generality. Rewrite the list beginning with the most general word or group of words and ending with the most specific.

natural poisonous substances
poisonous substances
mercury
substances

2   You will now find these words used in a paragraph. Read the paragraph and choose the most suitable title from the following:

a   Poison in rivers and the sea.
b   Natural poisonous substances.
c   Plants, forests and fish.

[1]The world is full of poisonous substances. [2]Many of these occur quite naturally, independently of any action of man. [3]Thus the vapours from an active volcano may contain so much sulphur that plants cannot grow nearby. [4]Rivers flowing through forests may become deoxygenated because so much natural organic material is deposited in them. [5]Mercury, occurring naturally in the ocean, may reach such high levels that large numbers of fish are killed.

3   The sentences in the paragraph are numbered. Write down the numbers of the sentences that refer to the following:
   a   poisonous substances in general
   b   natural poisonous substances
   c   specific kinds of natural poisonous substances.

Write down the numbers of the sentences that refer to:
   d   what is true in general
   e   what is possible.

4   Show the relationships between the different levels of generality in the passage by completing the following table.

Level 1

Level 2

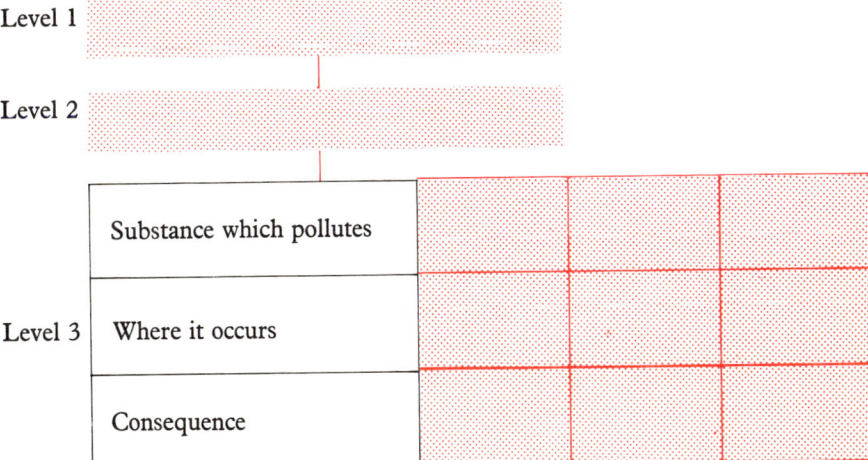

Unit 2 GENERALIZATIONS

Activity 4

1 The following statements have different levels of generality. Read them carefully and order them according to their level. Each statement contains one idea, or **proposition.** Note that two propositions may have the same level of generality.

a   The culture of medieval Europe did not change much.
b   Some cultures change rapidly.
c   Culture patterns change.
d   Cultures have definite patterns.
e   Some culture changes are slow.
f   In modern times cultural patterns have changed quickly.

2 You will now find these statements used in a paragraph. Read the paragraph and write down the numbers of the sentences that contain more than one of the above propositions.

[1]Cultures have definite patterns. [2]But these patterns are modified as they are transmitted from one generation to the next. [3]Sometimes these changes take place slowly and sometimes they are rapid. [4]The medieval era was for Western civilization a period of fairly slow change in culture patterns, while the modern period has been characterized by rapid and dramatic changes. [5]However, in spite of these changes, a coherent pattern remains.

3 Choose the sentence which best summarizes the paragraph.
   a   Culture patterns change at different rates.
   b   Some cultures change more rapidly than others.
   c   Cultures have patterns which change but remain coherent.
   d   Culture patterns are transmitted from one generation to the next.

4 Decide which of the following statements are, according to the passage, true in general and which are only true in some cases.

Part 4 LEVELS OF GENERALITY EXPRESSED BY PROBABILITY, FREQUENCY AND QUANTITY

    a   Cultures have definite patterns.
    b   Culture patterns are modified.
    c   Culture patterns change rapidly.
    d   Culture patterns are transmitted to the next generation.
    e   Culture patterns change slowly.

5   Choose the diagram which best expresses the structure of the paragraph.

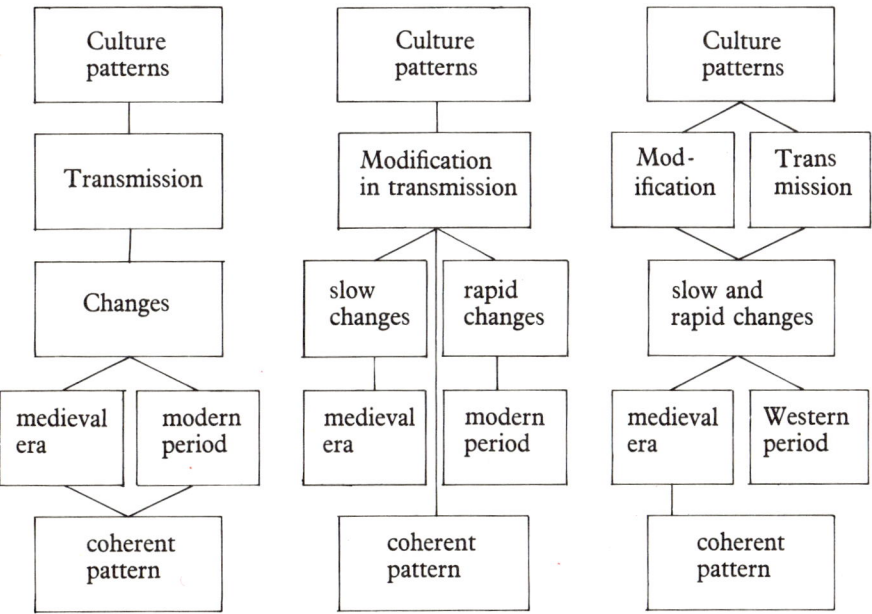

**Part 4
Levels of generality expressed by probability, frequency and quantity**

We have seen that passages may contain statements with different levels of generality. We are now going to study ways of making generalizations of different levels by using expressions of probability, frequency and quantity. The most general statements cover 100% of cases. Here are two equally general statements about snakes:

Snakes are cold-blooded.
Snakes are not warm-blooded.

We can also give the same information by using expressions of frequency and quantity.

Unit 2 GENERALIZATIONS

FREQUENCY	QUANTITY
Snakes are always cold-blooded	All snakes are cold-blooded
Snakes are never warm-blooded	No snakes are warm-blooded

Now study these statements about snakes which are less general than the statements above.

DEGREE

PROBABILITY	FREQUENCY	QUANTITY
A person bitten by a mamba will probably die.	The mamba venom is usually fatal.	Most mamba bites are fatal.
	The king cobra often attacks people.	Many king cobras attack people.
A cobra bite may be fatal.	A cobra bite is sometimes fatal.	Some cobra bites are fatal.
It is unlikely that a viper bite will be fatal.	A viper bite is rarely fatal.	Few viper bites are fatal.

Notice how the degree of probability, frequency and quantity decreases towards the bottom of the table.

Activity 5

This activity shows how expressions of probability, frequency and quantity can be used to make statements with different levels (degrees) of generality about data obtained in an investigation.

A teacher at a university made a survey to find out whether his students needed English; and if so, what they needed it for. Study the table giving his results and read the paragraph of the teacher's report.

Part 4 LEVELS OF GENERALITY EXPRESSED BY PROBABILITY, FREQUENCY AND QUANTITY

PURPOSE	%AGE OF STUDENTS	
	Economics	Engineering
Reading textbooks	80	90
Reading journals	60	70
Reading legal documents	5	1
Reading business letters	40	20
Writing reports	25	10
Writing letters	5	7
Filling in application forms	6	10
Attending lectures	60	40
Attending seminars	5	10
Talking to English-speaking visitors	6	8
Giving lectures	0	0

Students in this university need English for a variety of purposes. Most require an ability to read textbooks, and some attend lectures. 90% of engineering students, for example, read textbooks in English and 60% of economics students attend lectures in English.

Expressions of probability, frequency and quantity can be used to show approximate proportion. Complete the following paragraphs using expressions given in each list.

1   Economics students need to be able to read in English. ...... read textbooks and ...... read journals of economics in English. Writing is much less important. ...... write reports in English but ...... need English to write letters.

many
some
most
few

2   There is a range of purposes for which engineering students need English. They ...... have to read journals and they ...... attend lectures in English. It is ......, however, that they will attend seminars in English.

unlikely
may
probably
possible

Unit 2 GENERALIZATIONS

3   It is clear that English is necessary for the majority of students for many purposes apart from reading textbooks. They ...... read journals in English and they ...... have to read business letters. Although they ...... attend seminars in English, they ...... attend lectures in English.

often
rarely
seldom
very often
sometimes

Notice that the following three sentences refer to approximately the same proportion of cases.

Most engineering students have to read journals in English.
Engineering students usually have to read journals in English.
Engineering students probably have to read journals in English.

Look again at the tables at the beginning of this part containing statements about snakes. We can group the expressions according to the proportion of cases to which they refer as follows:

PROBABILITY	FREQUENCY	QUANTITY
probably	usually	most
	often	many
may/possible	sometimes	some
unlikely	rarely	few

100%

0%

Activity 6

Read each of the following paragraphs and decide how many levels of generality they contain.

PARAGRAPH 1

Most airline pilots require a knowledge of English. Although few need English to deal with emergencies, a knowledge of English for these situations is a wise safety measure. Some have to deal with English-speaking colleagues.

Part 4 LEVELS OF GENERALITY EXPRESSED BY PROBABILITY, FREQUENCY AND QUANTITY

PARAGRAPH 2

Many parents find it hard to accept the idea of their children getting married. Some parents become so attached to their children that they do not like the idea of giving them up. Some need to have a child at home who depends on them so that they can feel they have a place in the world.

PARAGRAPH 3

Firms always need statistics. They usually need to calculate the average wage of their employees. In addition, companies sometimes need to determine statistically whether consumers like a new product.

PARAGRAPH 4

It is unlikely that a personal assistant will be successful in her career without a knowledge of English. She may need it for translating business letters. She will probably need it as well for arranging appointments with English-speaking clients.

Now rewrite each paragraph, referring to the same proportion of cases. Make the following changes:

Paragraph 1
Replace the expressions of quantity by expressions of probability.

Example: Most airline pilots require a knowledge of English.
It is probable that airline pilots will require a knowledge of English.

Paragraph 2
Replace the expressions of quantity by expressions of frequency.

Paragraph 3
Replace the expressions of frequency by expressions of quantity.

Paragraph 4
Replace the expressions of probability by expressions of quantity.

Unit 2 GENERALIZATIONS

**Part 5
Application of
reading strategies**

The following passage contains different levels of generalizations. First, look at this diagram which presents information from the passage visually. Then use the diagram to answer the questions which follow it.

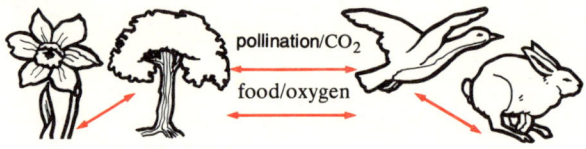

1   What do plants obtain from animals?
2   How do plants depend on animals?
3   Can you think of examples of relations between animals?
4   Can you think of examples of relations between plants?

The answers to the questions will provide you with a prediction of the main content of the passage.

Now choose one item from the following list and read the passage rapidly in order to obtain the relevant information.

1   The purpose of ecology.
2   The way in which ecologists consider man.
3   Ways in which animals affect each other.
4   The effects plants have on other plants.

Now read the passage again paragraph by paragraph in order to answer the comprehension questions. If you have difficulty in understanding the passage, the language study questions in the margins may help you. However, you do not need to answer all the language study questions yet.

THE SCOPE OF ECOLOGY

No living creature, plant or animal, can exist in complete isolation. An animal[1] is bound to depend on other living creatures, ultimately plants, for its food supply; it must also depend upon the activities of plants for a continued oxygen

[1] Does this refer to animals in general or to a particular animal?

Part 5 APPLICATION OF READING STRATEGIES TO A PASSAGE WITH DIFFERENT LEVELS OF GENERALITY

[2] There are two examples of *its* and one example of *it* in this sentence. Do they refer to the same thing?

supply for its respiration.[2] Apart from these two basic relationships[3] it may be affected directly or indirectly in countless different ways by other plants and animals around it. Other animals prey on it or compete with it for the same food; plants may provide shelter, concealment or nesting material, and so on. Similarly, the animal will produce its own effects on the surrounding plants and animals: some it may eat or destroy, for others it will provide food;[4] and through its contribution of manure it may influence the texture and fertility of the soil.

[3] Which two basic relationships have just been mentioned?

[4] What do *some* and *others* refer to?

1   Complete the following table to show the levels of generality expressed in the paragraph.

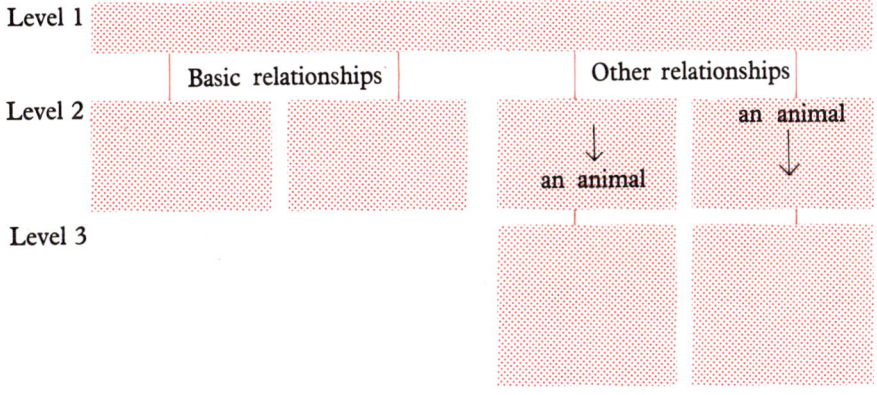

This dependence on other living things is not confined to animals.[5] Though plants manufacture their own food by photosynthesis, they are dependent on animal respiration for at least a part of the carbon dioxide which they use as raw material in this process.[6] Supplies of mineral salts which they use to build up their substance can only be maintained through the activities of fungi and bacteria breaking down the organic matter left in the soil by other living creatures.[7] Again,[8] many plants are entirely dependent on animals for pollination or for the dispersal of their seeds. Moreover,[9] despite the apparently peaceful relationships in plant communities, there is intense competition going on for water, nutrient salts, and above all, for light.

[5] Does *this dependence* refer to all the relationships mentioned in paragraph 1 or some of them?

[6] Which process?

[7] What maintains supplies of mineral salts?

[8–9] Which of the following relationships do *again* and *moreover* express?
a   consequence
b   contrast
c   addition

Unit 2 GENERALIZATIONS

2   Suggest a title for the paragraph.
3   List the processes for which plants need other living things.
4   The final sentence in the paragraph concerns:
   a   relations between plants
   b   dependence of plants on animals
   c   peaceful relationships in plant communities.

We see, then, that other plants and animals, through their effects both direct and indirect, form an integral part of the environment of every living organism.¹⁰ In a well-defined community, such as exists in a wood, or a pond,¹¹ the population of plants and animals is influenced not only by physical factors like light, temperature, or humidity, but also by the complex interrelationships between the living creatures themselves. As a result, the population of different competing species exists in a state of delicate balance easily swayed¹² by the slightest change in any factor.

¹⁰ This sentence
a   follows the previous paragraph, chronologically.
b   is in contrast to the previous paragraphs.
c   summarizes the previous paragraphs.

¹¹ What are *a wood* and *a pond* examples of?

¹² Species exist in a state of balance or equilibrium. If there is a change in one of the factors which influence the species, the state of balance may be swayed ∴ what can we deduce as the meaning of *swayed*?

5   What kinds of factors influence a community?
6   What is the consequence of these influences?

Ecology thus seeks to explain these interrelationships between all the different members of a community as a whole. To the ecologist the reactions and behaviour of any plant or animal are like a piece of jigsaw puzzle:¹³ he must find out how it¹⁴ fits into the picture of the whole community. Man is seen in perspective as just another piece in this grand jigsaw, and his activities in terms of the effects, good or bad, that they are likely to produce on the communities and soils from which he derives his food.¹⁵

¹³ This is a jigsaw puzzle. For the ecologist what forms the pieces? What is the whole puzzle?

¹⁴ What must the ecologist fit into the picture of the whole community?

¹⁵ Complete these statements:
Man is seen as a ....
His activities...... in terms of their effects.
(Notice that the verb *is seen* is not repeated in the passage.)

7   In what ways are living things like pieces of a jigsaw puzzle?

The whole complex of the plants and animals forming a community, together with all the interacting physical factors of the environment, really forms a single unit, which has been called an

30

Part 5 APPLICATION OF READING STRATEGIES TO A PASSAGE WITH DIFFERENT LEVELS OF GENERALITY

[16] What does an ecosystem consist of?

ecosystem.[16] It will be seen that the final aim of ecology—the complete understanding of ecosystems—is an ideal one can scarcely hope to attain.[17] It is nevertheless an ideal well worth pursuing and valuable progress has been made towards it.

[17] What is the final aim of ecology?

Adapted from: Maurice Ashby *Plant Ecology* (Macmillan Company of Canada Ltd 1963) by permission of Macmillans, London and Basingstoke

8   According to this paragraph, the aim of ecology is:
    a   realistic and valuable
    b   idealistic and a waste of time
    c   idealistic but valuable.

WRITING A SUMMARY

Order the following statements from the passage according to their level of generality.

a   Plants need animal respiration for the manufacture of food.
b   Animals depend on plants and other animals in many ways.
c   Living creatures cannot exist in complete isolation.
d   Plants depend on other plants and on animals.
e   Other plants and animals form part of the environment of every living organism.
f   Animals depend on plants for their food supply.

Now write the statements in the form of a paragraph beginning with the most general. Use each of the following connectors once: *in addition, for example, similarly.*

Unit 3 Descriptions

Preview
This unit practises understanding how information is organized in descriptive passages.

Part 1
draws attention to some of the purposes of descriptions and to some characteristics which descriptions include.

Part 2
is concerned with descriptions of substances and their properties.

Part 3
contains descriptions of processes and their stages.

Part 4
deals with ordering information in descriptive passages.

Part 5
provides practice in applying reading strategies to a complex description.

Part 1 DESCRIPTIONS AND THEIR PURPOSES

**Part 1
Descriptions and
their purposes**

Read the following descriptions rapidly and answer the questions after them.

This toadstool is dangerous

The Deathcap is the most poisonous of all toadstools. It is found in woods in autumn. It has a white stalk and a white cap at the base. This distinguishes it from edible toadstools. After the Deathcap has been eaten 6-15 hours can pass before signs of poisoning appear. By this time it is too late and certain death will follow.

a

Great Vampire Bat (desmodus rotundus)

Distribution: from Mexico to Paraguay. Nocturnal. Owes its name to its habit of feeding on blood. The bat punctures the skin of its victim with its upper incisors. The bat's saliva prevents the blood from coagulating.

b

Hafnium: Very strong absorbing power for thermal neutrons. Extremely good resistance to water at elevated temperatures - even better than zirconium. Good resistance to irradiation damage. High melting point (2130°C).

Beryllium: Very low density ($1.85 \, g \, cm^{-3}$). Very low neutron absorption characteristics. Excellent thermal conductivity. High specific heat (higher than any other structural metal). Very readily penetrated by X-rays.

d

Pottery funerary urn

Panshan type

Excavated in Kansu province, Eastern China.

Neolithic period, circa 2000 BC.

Painted with zig-zag designs.

e

Give yourself a
NIKKAX
and see what it gives you

Tough steel body designed for strength yet light enough for comfort.

Wide range of interchangeable lenses.

Built-in exposure meter.

Slim, elegant carrying-case.

Smooth noiseless mechanism.

Pictures at the tips of your fingers

c

Unit 3   DESCRIPTIONS

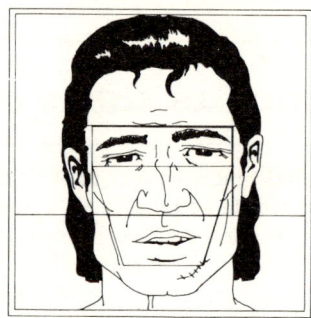

Wanted for Murder

MAN   between 27 and 33   about 5 feet 6 inches
medium build   heavy shoulders
hair brown brushed back   broken nose

If you think you have any information about this man,

contact any police station.

f

1   Suggest a purpose for each of the above descriptions.
2   What is each one describing?
3   Which are **a** notices, **b** advertisements, **c** extracts from books?
4   Which mention **a** dimensions, **b** behaviour, **c** colour, **d** physical properties?

There are many types of descriptions and different purposes of descriptions. There are, for example, descriptions of living things, objects, and substances. Each type includes particular characteristics. In this unit we will study some of the main types of descriptions and the characteristics they include.

**Part 2
Descriptions
of substances
and their properties**

In Part 1 we saw that descriptions can have different purposes and contain different characteristics. Below is a passage which describes a substance and refers to its various characteristics.

Part 2 DESCRIPTIONS OF SUBSTANCES AND THEIR PROPERTIES

1 Read the whole passage rapidly in order to answer these questions concerning specific details:

    a   What is the proportion of carbon in the earth's crust?
    b   Where are diamonds found?

2 Read the passage again paragraph by paragraph in order to answer the comprehension questions. Use the language study questions in the margins to help you understand the paragraphs.

CARBON

Carbon is a solid non-metallic chemical element (symbol C) occurring in the pure crystalline form as[1] diamond and graphite. It is also found in the combined form as a constituent of all organic materials, including coal and petroleum,[2] and of inorganic compounds such as limestone and baking powder. Despite its wide distribution, carbon constitutes only 0.19 per cent of the earth's crust.

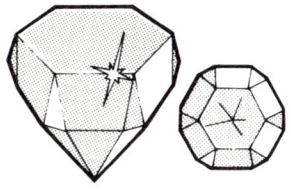

[1]
as here means:
a in the form of
b since
c similar to.

[2]
This means:
a carbon includes coal and petroleum.
b organic materials contain coal and petroleum.
c coal and petroleum are examples of organic materials.

1 Summarize the paragraph by completing the following diagram.

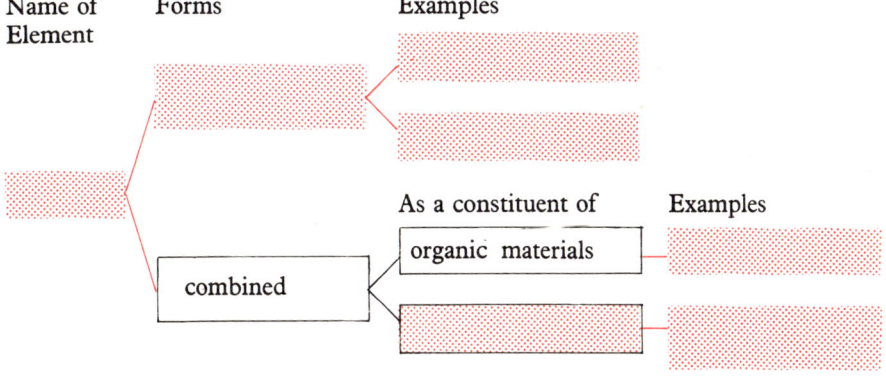

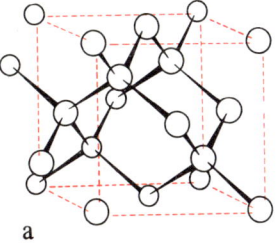

a

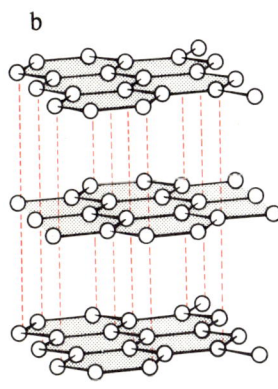

b

Which diagram represents the structure of diamond and which represents that of graphite?

The two elementary forms of carbon[3] have very different properties. In diamond the atoms are so tightly bound one to another that it provides man with his hardest[4] known substance. On the other hand, the second crystalline form of carbon, graphite, is a soft black substance with atoms hexagonally arranged in parallel sheets.[5] Each

[3]
Which are the two elementary forms?

[5]
Hard is the opposite of
....
...... is the opposite of *tight*.

35

Unit 3   DESCRIPTIONS

[6] The word *that* appears twice in this sentence. What does it refer to each time?

[7] What gives graphite its slippery feeling and explains its uses mentioned?

sheet is only loosely bound to that above and to that below it,[6] giving graphite a slippery feeling and explaining its use as a lubricant and in writing instruments.[7] The 'lead' of lead pencils is basically graphite. Another important difference between diamond and graphite is that of electrical conductivity. Diamond is a non-conductor while graphite conducts in the direction parallel to the hexagonal sheets. Both have high melting and boiling points.

2 Complete the following table to show what determines the properties given in the table.

SUBSTANCE	MOLECULAR STRUCTURE	PROPERTY
diamonds		hard
graphite		soft

∴ these properties depend on ......

3 In what other ways are diamond and graphite different? In what ways are they similar?

The optical properties of diamond are extremely significant. It has the highest index of refraction of any familiar gemstone and therefore reflects more light back to the eye than any other gem.[8] It also has remarkable dispersive power:[9] the light is broken up into the colours of the spectrum. These optical factors combined with the unusual clarity and transparency of the mineral, give the diamond its brilliance. Over 90% of the world's diamonds come from South Africa where they are found in kimberlite rock in the craters of extinct volcanoes. It takes several tons of kimberlite obtained from the earth by mining methods to yield a fraction of a carat of perfect diamond.[10] The popular interest in diamonds concentrates on their value as gemstones, but the stones have greater value as industrial tools. Industrial diamond tools may be used to drill or shape glass and ceramic articles and to grind and polish steels. Artificial diamonds have been produced by heating and

[8] What explains diamond's ability to reflect so much light back to the eye?

[9] What phrase explains the meaning of *dispersive power*?

[10] Diamonds are found in kimberlite rock. Several tons of kimberlite are necessary to yield a fraction of a carat of perfect diamond. ∴ what does *yield* mean in this context?

36

Part 2 DESCRIPTIONS OF SUBSTANCES AND THEIR PROPERTIES

compressing carbon in the form of graphite or carbon-containing compounds such as carbohydrates.[11]

11
What are needed in order to produce artificial diamonds?
a   Graphite, carbon-containing compounds and carbohydrates.
b   Either graphite or a carbon-containing compound.
c   Graphite and carbohydrates.

4   What optical properties of diamonds are mentioned?

5   Choose the best title for the paragraph:
   a   Diamonds as gemstones and in industry.
   b   The optical properties of diamonds.
   c   The occurrence and properties of diamonds.

12
At high temperatures carbon reacts, but at low temperatures, it is inert. What can you deduce as the meaning of *inert*?

At low temperatures all forms of carbon are relatively inert,[12] but at elevated temperatures will combine with oxygen to form oxides. Any form of carbon when combined with a large quantity of oxygen at an elevated temperature forms carbon monoxide. Carbon monoxide is also formed in the incomplete combustion of petroleum products and is found in appreciable percentages in the automobile exhaust.[13] Elementary carbon, when heated in an atmosphere of excess oxygen, is converted to the dioxide. Carbon dioxide is moderately non-reactive. Materials which burn at relatively low temperature, such as wood, petroleum products and paper,[14] do not continue to burn in CO_2. For this reason carbon dioxide is used as a fire-suppressing agent in fire extinguishers.[15] Carbon is stable towards water but undergoes slight oxidation when heated with the oxidizing acids.[16] In reaction with alkali, however, it does not suffer any attack.

13
What is found in an automobile exhaust?

14
What are wood, petroleum products and paper examples of?

15
Why is CO_2 used as a fire-suppressing agent?

16
An oxidizing acid is an acid which causes oxidation. Carbon undergoes oxidation when heated with these acids. ∴ *carbon undergoes oxidation* means:
a   carbon causes oxidation
b   carbon suffers oxidation
c   carbon combines with oxidation.

Reprinted with permission from Collier's Encyclopedia © 1963 Crowell-Collier Publishing Company

6   Suggest a title for the paragraph.
7   Complete the following table to show how carbon combines with oxygen.

FORM OF CARBON	AMOUNT OF OXYGEN	RESULT
any form		

Unit 3   DESCRIPTIONS

8   In what two ways is carbon monoxide produced?

We can now summarize the main features found in descriptions of substances as follows: forms, occurrence, structure, properties, reactions, uses.

Complete the following sentences which express each of the features using information from the passage.

Forms: There are two forms of carbon ......
Occurrence: Diamonds are found in ......
Structure: In graphite atoms are arranged ......
Properties: Diamond is ...... whereas graphite is ......
Reactions: At elevated temperatures carbon combines with ... to form ......

Uses: Diamonds can be used for ...... while graphite is used as ......

Activity 1

Describing a substance
Study the following information in note form about silicon.

Manufacture of chemically resistant steel.
Attacked by halogens and by oxygen when heated.
Hard, brittle.
Not in uncombined form: silicates and silicon dioxide.
Most rocks contain silicates.
Diamond-like crystal structure.

Now write a short paragraph using the information and arranging it in the following order: forms, occurrence, structure, properties, reactions, uses.

**Part 3
Descriptions of processes and their stages**

Part 2 studied descriptions of substances and their properties. This part considers the ways in which processes are described.

Part 3 DESCRIPTIONS OF PROCESSES AND THEIR STAGES

Read the following passage about coffee in order to find out where coffee is processed and where it is roasted. The language study questions in the margins may help you to understand the passage.

COFFEE AND ITS PROCESSING

The coffee plant, an evergreen shrub or small tree of African origin, begins to produce fruit 3 or 4 years after being planted. The fruit is hand-gathered when it is fully ripe and a reddish purple in colour. The ripened fruits of the coffee shrubs are processed where they are produced to separate the coffee seeds from their covering and from the pulp.[1] Two different techniques are in use: a wet process and a dry process.

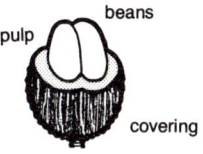

[1] What is the purpose of the processing?

The wet process First the fresh fruit is pulped by a pulping machine.[2] Some pulp still clings to the coffee, however, and this residue is removed by fermentation in tanks. The few remaining traces of pulp are then removed by washing. The coffee seeds are then dried to a moisture content of about 12 per cent either by exposure to the sun or by hot-air driers. If dried in the sun, they must be turned by hand several times a day for even drying.[3]

[2] The coffee seeds are separated from the pulp by a pulping machine.
∴ *pulp* in this context means: ...... the pulp from the seeds.

The dry process In the dry process the fruits are immediately placed to dry either in the sun or in hot-air driers. Considerably more time and equipment is needed for drying than in the wet process. When the fruits have been dried to a water content of about 12 per cent the seeds are mechanically freed from their coverings.

[3] The beans must be turned so that parts of the bean are given the same exposure. ∴ *even* means:
a divisible by two
b flat
c equally balanced
d calm.

1 Complete the following diagram to show the different stages of the wet process.

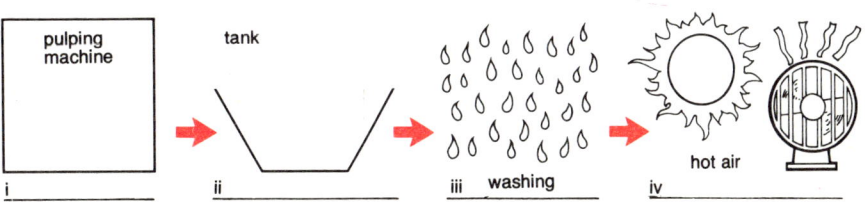

Unit 3 DESCRIPTIONS

2   Give examples of stages which are:
    a   manual
    b   mechanized.
3   What is the disadvantage of the dry process?
4   What stages in the wet process are not included in the dry process?

The characteristic aroma and taste of coffee only appear later and are developed by the high temperatures to which they are subjected during the course of the process known as roasting.[4] Temperatures are raised progressively to about 220–230°C. This releases steam, carbon dioxide, carbon monoxide and other volatiles from the beans,[5] resulting in a loss of weight of between 14 and 23 per cent. Internal pressure of gas expands the volume of the coffee seeds from 30 to 100 per cent. The seeds become rich brown in colour; their texture becomes porous and crumbly under pressure. But the most important phenomenon of roasting is the appearance of the characteristic aroma of coffee, which arises from very complex chemical transformations within the beans. The coffee, on leaving the industrial roasters,[6] is rapidly cooled in a vat where it is stirred and subjected to cold air propelled by a blower. Good quality coffees are then sorted by electronic sorters to eliminate the seeds that roasted badly. The presence of seeds which are either too light or too dark depreciates the quality.[7]

[5] What releases steam, etc.?

[4] At what stage do the characteristic aroma and taste of coffee appear?

[6] Does the cooling take place before, after or during the roasting?

[7] What causes seeds to be too light or too dark?

Adapted from: 'Coffee Production' in *Encyclopaedia Britannica*, 15th edition (1974), by permission of Encyclopaedia Britannica, Inc.

5   Complete the following diagrams to show cause/effect relationships.

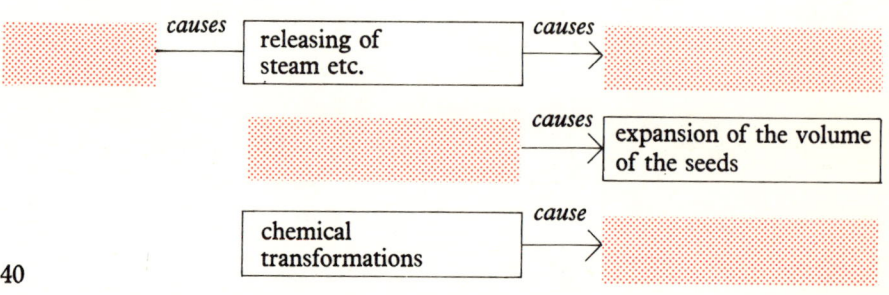

Changes

[ ] *causes* → releasing of steam etc. *causes* → [ ]

[ ] *causes* → expansion of the volume of the seeds

chemical transformations *cause* → [ ]

40

Part 4 WAYS OF ORDERING INFORMATION IN DESCRIPTIVE PASSAGES

6   What other changes during roasting are mentioned?
7   What is the importance of roasting?

We can summarize the main aspects found in descriptions of processes as follows:

Series of activities which determine the different stages of the process.
Sequence of the stages.
Changes occurring from one stage to another.
Purpose of the process and of the different stages.
Method of performing the activities.
Equipment or components used.

Activity 2

Read the following sentences which express some of the aspects included in descriptions of processes. Identify the main aspect expressed in each sentence.

1   Pulping, drying and roasting are basic to coffee processing.
2   In the dry process seeds are separated from their coverings after being dried.
3   The beans are dried either naturally by exposure to the sun or mechanically by hot-air driers.
4   The beans lose weight as a final result of being exposed to high temperatures.
5   The coffee is treated in industrial roasters and cooled in vats. Electronic sorters are used to eliminate the seeds that roasted badly.
6   Fermentation removes the residue of pulp from beans.

Part 4
Ordering information in descriptions

Part 3 studied a passage describing a process and its different stages. This part deals with ways of ordering information in descriptions. First look at the following pair of sentences:

1   Paper is made from wood pulp.
2   Wood pulp is used to make paper.

Unit 3   DESCRIPTIONS

The information in the two sentences is almost the same. The difference between them is the order in which the information is given.

The first element in sentence 1 is *paper*.
The first element in sentence 2 is *wood pulp*.
Sentence 1 gives us information about paper.
Sentence 2 gives us information about wood pulp.

The first element in the sentence we will call the **theme** of the sentence. So we can show the difference between the two sentences as follows:

1   Paper is made from wood pulp.
    Theme
2   Wood pulp is used to make paper.
    Theme

In the examples we are going to study, the theme is also the subject of the sentence. The subject can be one word (e.g. *paper*) or it can be a group of words (e.g. *wood pulp*).

Activity 3

Underline the theme in the following sentences.
Example: Other plant materials can be used to make paper.

1   Paper is often made from dry pulp sheets.
2   The dry pulp sheets are turned into wet pulp.
3   Various materials are added to the pulp.
4   The damp layers of pulp are pressed into a thin sheet.
5   The thin sheet is dried.

Activity 4

Some descriptions of processes concern a single substance, and describe the operations that are done to it and how the substance is transformed. In this type of passage the theme of each sentence is often the substance in its different states.

Underline the theme of each sentence in the following description. (Where a pronoun is used write the word or group of words to which it refers.)

Part 4 WAYS OF ORDERING INFORMATION IN DESCRIPTIVE PASSAGES

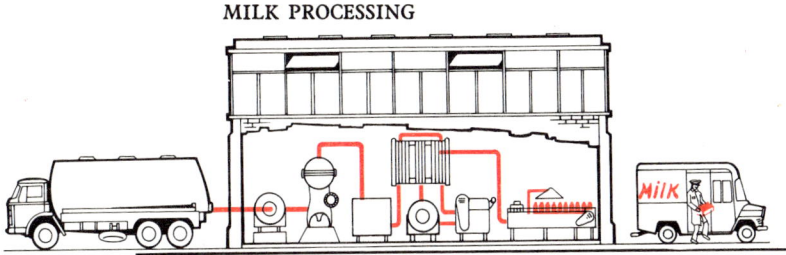

MILK PROCESSING

Milk is first received at the milk plant where three different operations are performed on it: grading, weighing and sampling. It is graded by examining it for abnormal odours and flavours. The milk is weighed by emptying it into a tank on scales. A sample of the milk is then taken and tested for butterfat.

The milk then flows to a clarifier whose purpose is to remove foreign material and sediment. The clarified milk may then be homogenized to prevent cream formation. The homogenized milk is then pasteurized to destroy all pathogenic bacteria. The pasteurized milk is cooled to 50°F or below. The cooled milk is then ready for distribution.

1   Using information in paragraph 1, complete this diagram to show the operations performed on milk.

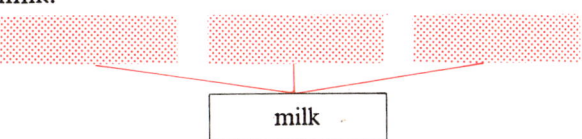

2   Using information in paragraph 2, complete this diagram to show each stage and its purpose.

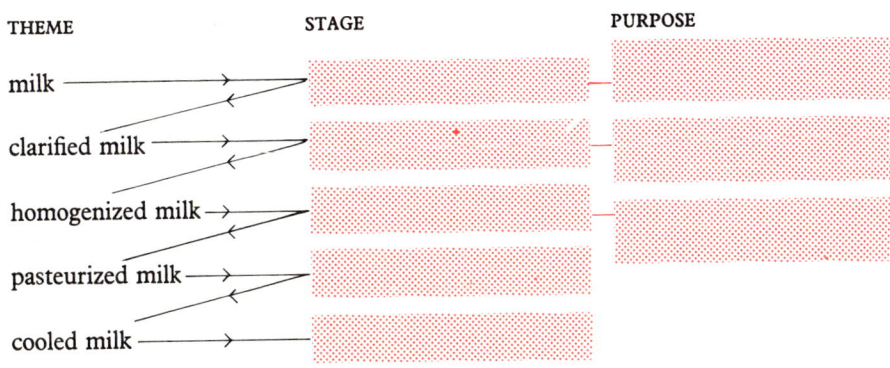

Unit 3 DESCRIPTIONS

Activity 5

Read the following passage and suggest a title for it. (The passage describes how protein foods can be produced by using paraffin as the nutrient source for the growth of yeast.)

Yeast is added to paraffin in a tank along with water, air, ammonia and mineral salts. The yeast cells feed on the paraffin and start to grow. The yeast solution then goes into a centrifuge where it is spun rapidly. The concentrated yeast, now thick and creamy, goes from the centrifuge to a container. It then passes into a drier where the cream is heated and the water evaporates. The purified yeast then appears as a fine powder. This yeast powder has a very high protein content. It does not have a very pleasant taste but could ultimately provide a very valuable food for man.

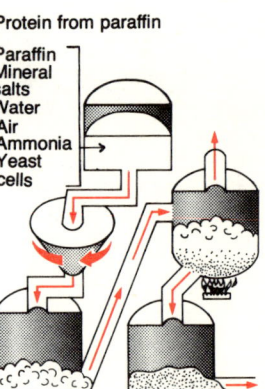

Protein from paraffin

Paraffin
Mineral salts
Water
Air
Ammonia
Yeast cells

Now complete the following diagram with the theme of each sentence. (Where a pronoun is used write the word or group of words to which it refers.)

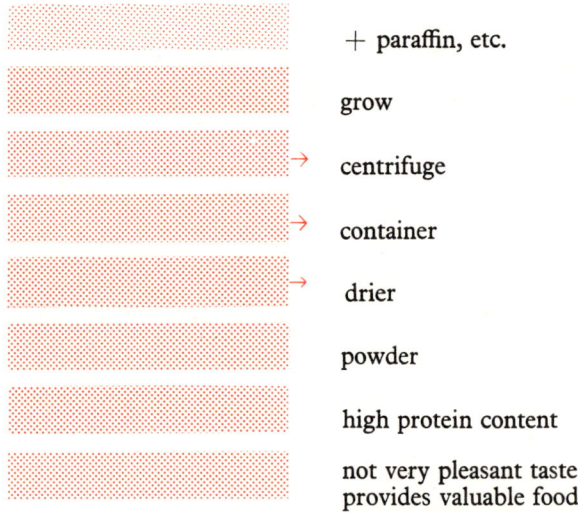

	+ paraffin, etc.
	grow
→	centrifuge
→	container
→	drier
	powder
	high protein content
	not very pleasant taste / provides valuable food

So far we have studied passages which describe the processes through which a single substance passes. We will now study how information is ordered in passages which refer to different substances, components or stages in a process.

Part 4 WAYS OF ORDERING INFORMATION IN DESCRIPTIVE PASSAGES

Study the following pair of sentences.

1   The pulp goes to the papermaking machine.
2   The papermaking machine consists of a series of rollers.

The theme in sentence 1 is *the pulp*.
The theme in sentence 2 is *the papermaking machine*.

Notice that the papermaking machine is the only element in sentence 2 that was mentioned in sentence 1. In a passage, the theme of each sentence is often the element of the sentence that was mentioned previously. The theme is therefore **known information**. The rest of the sentence is **new information**. We can show the known and the new information as follows:

The pulp goes to the papermaking machine.

The papermaking machine consists of a series of rollers.

(known information)   (new information)

Activity 6

Study the following passage. Underline the theme of each sentence and then circle the previous mention of the theme.

The milk goes first to a clarifier. The clarifier is a machine for applying centrifugal force. It consists of a rapidly revolving bowl containing several discs. The discs separate the milk into thin streams. The streams of milk then pass into a preheater. The preheater elevates the temperature of the milk to 130°F and then allows the milk to flow to the homogenizer. The homogenizer is a pump which is capable of exerting considerable pressure on the milk, thus forcing it through a restricted opening. The small size of the opening causes the milk to travel at high velocity. This causes a reduction in the size of the butterfat globules. The homogenizer thus prevents cream formation even after long standing.

Unit 3   DESCRIPTIONS

Activity 7

Study the following sentences about radio communication and label the diagram using words from the list given.

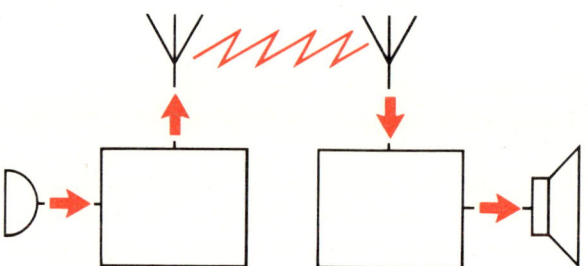

Microphone
Receiving aerial
Transmitter
Loudspeaker
Receiver
Transmitting aerial

A radio transmitter generates radio-frequency waves.
A transmitting aerial radiates the waves into space.
A receiving aerial intercepts a portion of the radiated waves.
The receiving aerial often consists of a piece of wire or a loop.
The wire conducts small electrical signals to the radio receiver.
The radio receiver selects and amplifies the signals.
The radio receiver contains a detector.
Audio signals are sent out by the detector.
An amplifier strengthens the audio signals.
A loudspeaker converts the amplified audio signal into sound waves.

Now complete the following description of the whole process. Make information previously mentioned the theme of each sentence.

The first element in radio communication is a radio transmitter which .... into space by a .... is intercepted .... a piece of wire or a loop. ... conducts small electrical signals to the radio receiver. ... by the .... The radio receiver.... The detector .... are strengthened .... by a loudspeaker into ....

**Part 5
Application of
reading strategies**

The following passage is a complex descriptive passage. It is complex because it concerns a variety of aspects which are relevant to the description of

Part 5 APPLICATION OF READING STRATEGIES TO A COMPLEX DESCRIPTION

a community. The passage describes a group of Indians living in a remote region of Colombia, South America. First make a list containing aspects that you would expect to find in the description of a primitive community. For example:

food
customs and beliefs

Then read the whole passage rapidly to find out which of the items in your list appear in the passage.

Next read the passage carefully, paragraph by paragraph, in order to answer the comprehension questions. This will enable you to summarize the main aspects of the description. You do not need to complete all of the language study questions in the margins yet.

THE NOANAMÁ

The Noanamá are a handsome people; tallish and well-built with the heavy chest and shoulders of men accustomed to rowing;[1] their dark hair in a bowl-like fringe around the head; light-skinned, narrow-nosed and high-cheekboned, mongoloid in appearance with penetrating dark eyes. The women are often beautiful, with long flowing black hair and wearing no more than a cloth about their waist. Sometimes they put 'bija', a red dye, on their faces, and flowers in their hair. For ceremonies they cover their bodies with blue 'jagua' dye in a series of designs.[2] But it is the men, especially the unmarried boys, who dress up for special occasions with magnificent silver pendants, strings of blue, orange, red and white porcelain beads which come from Panama, and are an indication of wealth—so many that they can scarcely move their heads from side to side.[3] Finally there is the glistening white shirt, a symbol of status and the only European garment[4] we ever saw them wearing.

1 Number the boxes in the following diagram to show the order in which the aspects of the description appear in the passage.

[1] The picture shows a man rowing. What physical characteristic of the Noanamá results from rowing?

[2] Who use blue 'jagua' dye?

[3] Why is it difficult for them to move their heads?
[4] Shirts (specific term) are a kind of garment (general term). Give other examples of garments.

Unit 3 DESCRIPTIONS

		men	women
PHYSICAL APPEARANCE			
clothes	ordinary		
	ceremonial		

2   What indicates:
    a   wealth
    b   status
    c   European influence?

3   a   What do women use to decorate themselves?
    b   What do men use?

[5] What does this sentence tell us about the Chocó region?

[7] What is not known about the Noanamá?

[8] This sentence gives us information about:
a   where they live
b   their origin
c   their legends.

[9] Which explanation is generally accepted?

These people, expert cultivators, hunters and fishermen, have lived in the river deltas and the coastal lowlands of Western Colombia—the Chocó—for hundreds of years.[5] They are a small tribe numbering probably no more than two thousand, speaking a language similar to that[6] of all the Indians living in the coastal lowlands from Ecuador to Panama. Where they came from, and when they arrived, remains a mystery.[7] Legend connects them with the pre-Conquest civilization of San Agustín.[8] Their characteristic pottery might suggest a link with pre-Inca Peru. Other considerations suggest that their earlier home lay in the Amazon basin and that at some time in the past they moved westwards across the Andes and finally halted by the Pacific (this is generally thought to be the case).[9] Yet[10] their appearance, their almost wholly water-based existence, even the habit of wearing flowers in their hair reminds one of faraway Polynesia.

[6] The writer is comparing the language of the Noanamá with the ...... of the Indians of other coastal lowlands.

[10] *Yet* indicates that what follows:
a   confirms the previous explanation
b   adds to the previous explanation
c   is in contrast to the previous explanation.

4   Complete the following table to summarize the theories concerning the origin of the Noanamá.

SUGGESTED TIME AND PLACE OF ORIGIN	EVIDENCE FOR THE THEORY
Pre-Conquest San Agustín	
	pottery

Part 5 APPLICATION OF READING STRATEGIES TO A COMPLEX DESCRIPTION

5 Which of the following descriptive aspects are mentioned in the paragraph: population, kinds of food, language, occupation, origin, how they travel, location, social structure?

Wherever they came from, they have lived in this region of the Chocó, between the lower parts of the río San Juan and the Pacific Ocean, for a very considerable time. Unlike the Indians of the highlands they were unaffected by the advance of the 'conquistadores'[11] which led to the break-up of the Andean tribes.[12] The forest, the heavy rains, the humid heat and the unhealthy swamps all discouraged the early explorers.[13] It was not until the relatively recent rise of Buenaventura as Colombia's major Pacific port[14] that the life of the Noanamá was disturbed by foreign influences.[15]

[11] Who were not affected by the advance of the conquistadores and who were affected?

[12] What was the result of this advance?

[13] Why did the conquistadores not reach the Chocó?

[14] What does the sentence tell us about Buenaventura?

[15] What caused the life of the Noanamá to be disturbed by foreign influence?

6 Complete the following table to summarize the information given about the Chocó.

| Location |
| Inhabitants |
| Climate |
| Physical Features |
| Economy |

To the Noanamá the river is the centre of activity. Men, women and children, at times whole families, move up and down the river in large and small canoes—some to their plantations, others fishing, or hunting up the numerous creeks[16] or transporting the great jars of ceremonial 'chicha' made from fermented maize.[17] Usually every member of the family has his own canoe. The children sometimes have small ones,[18] no more than eight feet long. There are also bigger canoes, perhaps twenty feet long or more, used for fishing or when the whole family embarks. Some Indians are particularly skilled in canoe-making. First, they select the tree,[19] often many miles away in

[16] The Noanamá go hunting in canoes up creeks. What can you deduce about the meaning of *creek*?

[17] The drink 'chicha' is kept in jars. ∴ a jar is a kind of ……

[18] What do the children have?

[19] This is the first stage of what process?

Unit 3 DESCRIPTIONS

[20] What does the sentence tell us about the meaning of *cedar*?

the forest—a cedar or similar resinous wood is preferable.[20] After they have cut it down, the trunk is floated through the creeks to the river. Then with axe and adze the canoe is shaped under a small shelter beside the riverside house. It may take more than a month for a man to make one, but once completed it lasts for years.

7 What activities mentioned are related to the river?

8 What are the main steps involved in making a canoe?

The Indians rise[21] as soon as it is light, the children run down to the river to swim, the women to the creek to bring fresh water. Soon maize soup is being prepared for breakfast. Before noon they eat again, usually fish, meat and bananas, the fruit of the 'chontaduro' palm and a drink of 'chicha'. When the sun has risen[22] over the river, some of the younger women with their children go by canoe to their distant forest plantation to collect maize, bananas and wild fruits. The older women stay in the house making pots which they use for drinking water and for 'chicha'. Later they have to prepare the evening meal and look after the children. The women do most of the daily work and each new day brings them much the same routine. The men, who may have been hunting during the night, pass the day repairing nets, replacing an arrow lost in their hunting, fishing with hook and line or 'atarraya' net.[23] In January after the rains, both men and women go to the forest plantation to sow maize. Later in August and September, they sow a second crop. Four months after each sowing, the maize is ready for gathering by the women alone.[24] At nightfall the family congregates once again, and after the babies are asleep in their hammocks they discuss the day's events. A man picks up a flute and starts playing. Soon sleeping mats are spread out on the platforms and the house falls silent.

Adapted from: Moser and Tayler: *The Cocaine Eaters*, Longman 1965.

[21] In this context *rise* means:
a move upwards
b make a revolution
c get up.

[22] In this context *rise* means:
a increase in cost
b move upwards
c begin to exist.

[23] The context tells us that hooks, lines and nets are all used for . . . .

[24] The context tells us that *sow* means:
a gather a crop
b water a crop
c look after a crop
d plant the seeds of a crop.

Part 5   APPLICATION OF READING STRATEGIES TO A COMPLEX DESCRIPTION

9   List the kinds of food eaten.
10 List the activities that are performed by:
    a   men alone
    b   women alone
    c   children
    d   men and women together
    e   women and children.
11 Complete the following table to show when the activities mentioned take place:

ACTIVITY	WHEN IT TAKES PLACE
getting fresh water from the creek	
women and children go to the plantation	
hunting	
the rainy season	
gathering the maize	

WRITING A SUMMARY
Answer the following questions on the passage. Write your answers in complete statements so that they provide a summary of the passage.
1   Where do the Noanamá people live?
2   Where are they generally believed to have originated?
3   Why have they only recently been disturbed by foreign influence?
4   What are their activities centred on?
5   How do they obtain their food? (By .... and cultivating ....)

Unit 4 Definitions

Preview
This unit is concerned with the use of definitions to convey information in passages.

Part 1
draws attention to the nature of definitions and how they are used in communication.

Part 2
deals with different types of definitions.

Part 3
practises ways of expressing definitions.

Part 4
shows how simple definitions can be expanded in paragraphs.

Part 5
provides practice in applying reading strategies to a passage concerned with the definition of several concepts.

Part 1
The nature of definitions

Read the following passage in order to find out about the device shown in the picture. Then answer the questions after the passage.

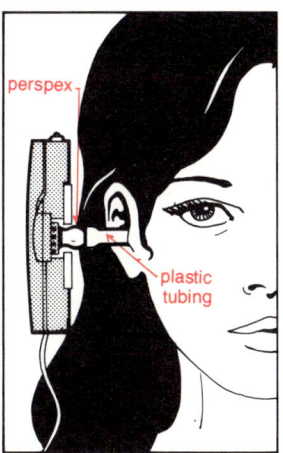

Methods have recently been elaborated to measure food crushing sounds so that foods can be manufactured to produce the exact level of noise considered desirable. After a considerable amount of preliminary study a technique was developed which records the sounds of food being masticated. The instrument is similar to a transistorized hearing aid and is inserted in the ear of the experimenter. The hearing aid picks up the noise produced and transmits it via an appropriate circuit to a magnetic tape and the recording is subsequently analysed for frequency and amplitude.

Use the diagram to answer these questions.
1   What does the masticometer consist of?
2   What are its dimensions?
3   How much does it weigh?

Now use the passage to answer these questions.
4   What is its function?
5   Where is it placed?
6   What does it resemble?
7   How does it work?

The masticometer is an instrument. In order to define it we have to choose the characteristic which makes it different from other members of the same class (other instruments; for example, a barometer or a stethoscope). Which of the following statements expresses the defining characteristic of a masticometer?

a   It is 5 cm long and weighs 20 grams.
b   It consists of an amplifier and a plastic tube.
c   It is connected to a magnetic tape.
d   It measures food crushing sounds.
e   It is used in experiments on food.

∴ we can define a masticometer as an instrument which ......

Unit 4 DEFINITIONS

In making a definition we normally give:
a   the specific concept being defined
b   the class to which the specific concept belongs
c   the specific characteristics of the concept which make it different from other members of the same class.

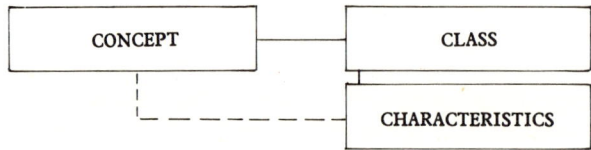

Use the following diagram to write a definition of an amplifier

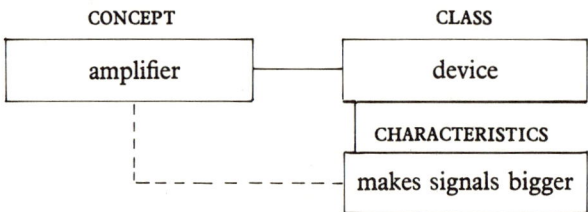

An amplifier ......

Notice that we can make a generalization about amplifiers in the following way:

An amplifier makes signals bigger.

Activity 1

Draw a diagram for each of the following statements to show whether it is a definition or a generalization.

1   A stethoscope is an instrument for studying sound generated inside the human body.
2   Hearing aids enable deaf people to hear sounds such as normal speech.
3   A frequency changer is a machine designed to receive power at one frequency and deliver it at another frequency.
4   Food technology is concerned with the processing of food.

Part 2
Types of definitions

Activity 2

We can identify two main types of definitions. The two types occur in the following passage. Read the passage carefully and then answer the questions concerning the definitions found in it.

Parasitology may be defined as the branch of biology which deals with the nature of parasitism and its effects on both the parasite and the host. Broadly defined, a parasite is an organism which lives for all or part of its life on or in another organism from which it derives some benefit, such as food, shelter or protection. Organisms living on the host are known as ectoparasites; those living within the host organism are called endoparasites.

1 Complete the following diagram to show the general and specific terms mentioned in the passage.

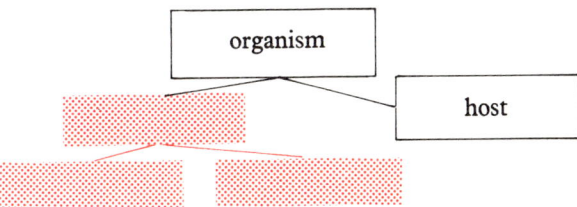

2 Which of the words in your diagram are defined in the passage?

3 What is the difference between the two kinds of parasites mentioned?

4 Complete the following diagrams to show the structure of two of the definitions in the passage.

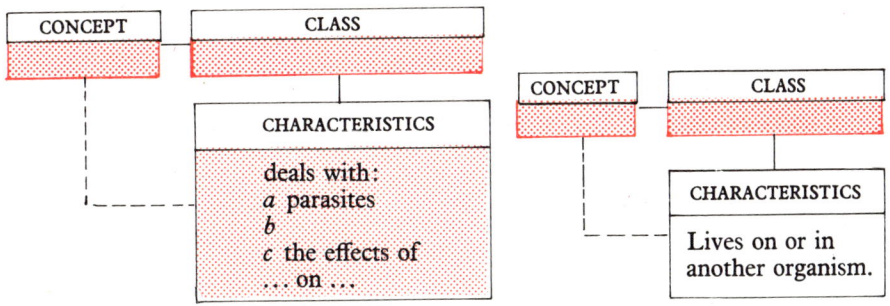

Notice that the structure of these definitions is:

| CONCEPT = CLASS + CHARACTERISTICS |

5   Use the information in the passage to complate the following diagram.

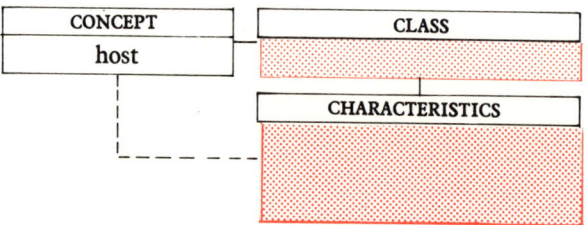

Now write a definition of *host* based on the diagram.

6   Identify the concept, the class and the characteristics in the following definition.

Organisms living on the host are known as ectoparasites.

This definition therefore has the structure:

| class + characteristics = name of concept |

We will call the definition with the structure

| concept = class + characteristics |

a real definition. A real definition specifies the nature of a concept. The nature is specified by giving the class and characteristics.

We will call definitions with the structure

| class + characteristics = name of concept |

nominal definitions. A nominal definition states the nature of a concept and then identifies it by giving its name.

Activity 3

This activity practises recognition of real and nominal definitions. Study the following passage and identify the definitions in it. Decide whether they are real or nominal definitions.

Part 2 TYPES OF DEFINITIONS

KINEMATICS
Kinematics is the branch of applied mathematics that deals with the motion of bodies without considering the forces which produce such motion. When a body moves, so changing its position, the distance it has moved is measured by the length of its path of motion. Distance is therefore a scalar quantity. Speed is also a scalar quantity. Speed is defined as the rate of change of distance with time. The speed of a body measured in a definite direction is known as its velocity. Consequently, velocity is a vector quantity. If there is a change in either the speed of a body or its direction of motion, then the body is subject to an acceleration. We may therefore define acceleration as the rate of change of velocity with time. When the speed of a body decreases with time the rate of decrease of speed is known as the deceleration.

Notice that the explicit markers used to express the two types of definitions are different:

real definitions	concept	*is defined as* / *may be defined as*	class + characteristics
nominal definitions	class + characteristics	*is known as* / *is called*	name of concept

Activity 4

This activity shows how the use of real and nominal definitions depends on the context.

Compare the following definitions:

1   Semantics is the branch of linguistics which studies meaning.
2   The branch of linguistics which studies meaning is called semantics.

In the first definition the theme is 'semantics'. What is the new information? In the second definition the theme is 'the branch of linguistics which studies meaning'. What is the new information?

Unit 4 DEFINITIONS

As we saw in Part 4 of Descriptions, an element of the sentence may be selected as theme because it has been mentioned previously in the same passage. Look again at the passage in Activity 2 of this unit. Find the two nominal definitions and identify the theme. Underline the part of the passage where the theme is mentioned previously.

Below are five sentences. Each sentence is followed by information in parentheses: (...). Use the information given in parentheses to write a definition. Make the information given in the preceding sentence the topic of your definition.

Example 1
The first communications satellites did not use stationary orbits.
(a stationary orbit = one in which the satellite travels round the earth once every 24 hours)

A stationary orbit is an orbit in which the satellite travels round the earth once every 24 hours.

Example 2
Orbits depend on gravitational attraction.
(a stationary orbit = one in which the satellite travels round the earth once every 24 hours)

An orbit in which the satellite travels round the earth once every 24 hours is known as a stationary orbit.

1   The first chapter of this book concerns cytology. (cytology = the science of cell structure)
2   Many people enjoy collecting coins. (numismatist = a person who collects coins)
3   Surveyors need to measure angles. (theodolite = an instrument for measuring angles)
4   Most countries have traditional stories and legends. (myths = traditional stories which often concern the supernatural)
5   Alcohol is produced by distillation. (distillation = process by which a liquid is evaporated and then condensed)

**Part 3
Ways of expressing defining characteristics**

In Part 2 we studied the two main types of definitions, real and nominal definitions. We saw that in real definitions the concept being defined is the theme. In nominal definitions the new information is the name of the concept. Thus the use of the two types of definitions depends on the context. In this part we will study ways of expressing one of the elements in definitions.

Activity 5

Study the following definitions concerned with chemistry and underline the part of each definition that refers to the characteristics.

1   Elements are chemical substances that cannot be broken down into anything simpler by chemical means.
2   A neutron is a particle having the same mass as a proton but carrying no electrical charge.
3   A trace is a substance used to follow a chemical reaction or a physical process.
4   Fractional distillation is the distillation process in which liquid mixtures are separated into their components.
5   A catalyst is a substance which accelerates a chemical reaction.
6   Cracking is the process by which large molecules are broken down into smaller ones by means of high temperatures and pressures.

Note that in the above statements the characteristics and the class are connected by means of certain relative words:

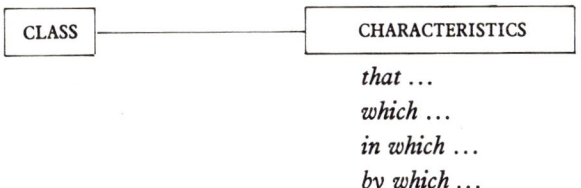

that ...
which ...
in which ...
by which ...

Notice *which* and *that* are omitted in the following:
(class)

X is a substance having ...... used for ......

Unit 4 DEFINITIONS

Activity 6

As we saw in Part 1 we can change a definition into a generalization by removing the class. For example,

definition	generalization
A catalyst is a substance which accelerates a chemical reaction.	A catalyst accelerates a chemical reaction.
A trace is a substance used to follow a chemical reaction or a physical process.	A trace is used to follow a chemical reaction or a physical process.

Now rewrite the following definitions as generalizations. The definitions all concern electronics.

1   A wafer is a piece of semiconductor used in transistors.
2   White noise can be defined as acoustic waves containing a wide range of adjacent random frequencies.
3   A parasitic aerial is an aerial which is not fed directly but which gains its energy by being close to a driven aerial.
4   Automatic frequency control (AFC) is a feedback circuit which controls the average radio frequency of an FM receiver.
5   A resistor is an electric component designed to introduce known resistance into a circuit.

Part 4
Expanded definitions

Part 3 studied different ways of expressing characteristics in definitions. Your attention was also drawn to the difference between definitions and generalizations. We are now going to study how definitions can be combined in a paragraph with descriptions, generalizations and examples.

Activity 7

Definitions expanded by descriptions
Study the following paragraph and underline the definition you find in it.

Part 4 EXPANDED DEFINITIONS

A telescope is an instrument for magnifying distant objects. It has two essential parts: the **objective** which collects light from the distant object and forms a real image, and the **eye-piece** which forms a magnified image of this image. Refracting telescopes use a convex lens as the objective and reflecting telescopes use a curved mirror of large diameter.

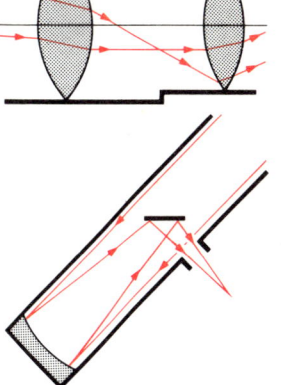

Which of the following pieces of information does the paragraph include?

a   function of telescopes
b   main structure of telescopes
c   invention of the telescope
d   function of the main parts of a telescope
e   some types of telescopes
f   different uses of the types of telescopes

Now complete the following diagram to show the structure of the information in the passage.

definition	general description		description of types	
	part	function	type	part

Use information in the passage to complete the following definitions.

A...... is a form of ...... which uses a convex lens as the objective.
A reflecting telescope is a ...... which uses a curved mirror ....

Activity 8

Definitions expanded by generalizations and examples
Read the following passage and say what concept is defined in it.

Man and most animals can only exist near the surface of the earth in the region known as the

Unit 4 DEFINITIONS

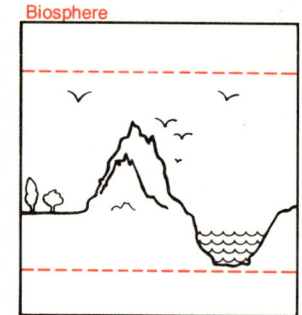

biosphere. The biosphere is the thin layer of soil, water and air in which all life exists. On land the biosphere only goes down as far as the deepest tree roots. In the sea most life is in the top 150 metres although the biosphere can be considered as extending to the depths of the ocean. Some birds and insects fly high into the sky, but most animals could not even live on the earth's highest mountains. The upper limit in the air can be estimated to be around 10 000 metres.

From: *Man's Environment* (Macdonald Visual Books)

Now complete the following diagram to show the structure of the information in the passage.

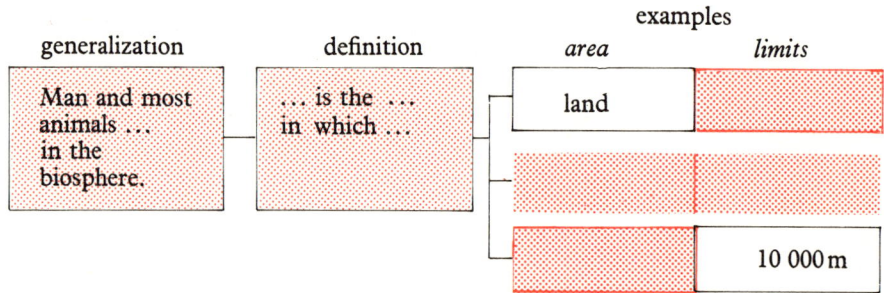

Activity 9

This activity practises another way of expanding a definition in a paragraph.

Read the following statements carefully.

1   Price elasticity of demand and supply is the responsiveness of demand to changes in price.
2   It is useful to be able to predict the extent to which a price change will affect supply and demand.
3   Supply and demand behave in the same way as the elastic in clothes.
4   A finance minister needs to know the degree to which a new tax will reduce demand.

Decide which of the statements is: a definition, a generalization, an example, and an analogy.

Part 5 APPLICATION OF READING STRATEGIES TO A PASSAGE CONCERNED WITH DEFINITIONS

You will now find the statements used in a paragraph. Read the paragraph and answer the questions which follow it.

ELASTICITY OF DEMAND AND SUPPLY
The elastic used in clothes extends and contracts under the influence of forces applied to it. Demand and supply similarly extend and contract under the influence of such forces as changes in price. It is often useful to know the degree of extension or contraction that will follow a given price change. For instance, a finance minister who is about to impose a tax of 10 per cent on some commodity with a view to raising revenue would like to know in advance the probable contraction in demand that this new tax will inevitably cause. The responsiveness of demand and supply to changes in price has been termed 'price elasticity of demand and supply'. Price elasticity of demand is the responsiveness of demand to changes in price. Price elasticity of supply is the responsiveness of supply to changes in price.
From: G Whitehead *Economics Made Simple*
(W H Allen and Co Ltd)

1   In what way are supply and demand similar to the elastic in clothes?
2   How will a price reduction affect demand?
3   Complete the following diagram to show the structure of the paragraph.

Part 5
Application of reading strategies

We are now going to study a passage which is concerned with the definition of a range of concepts. The passage is about systems and defines some of the concepts which are used in the systems approach to academic study. Here are some examples of things which are often considered as systems.

Unit 4 DEFINITIONS

the solar system

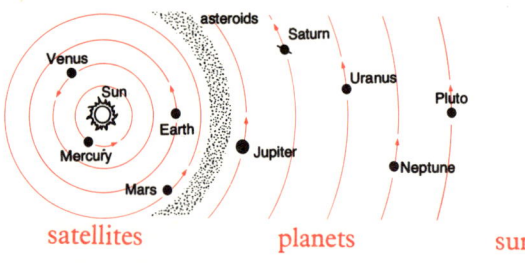

satellites   planets   sun

a factory

men   machines
buildings

Now answer these questions about the three systems. Your answers will help you to predict some of the content of the passage.

the heart

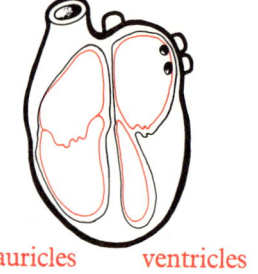

auricles   ventricles

1   What parts does each system consist of?
2   Which of the systems are natural and which is man-made?
3   When designing a system, such as a factory, what must be considered apart from the individual components?

Now read as much of the passage as necessary in order to find:

a   the traditional dictionary definition of system
b   the definition proposed by the writer.

Underline each definition when you find it.

Next read the passage carefully, paragraph by paragraph, and answer the comprehension questions. These will enable you to study how the different concepts related to systems are defined. The language study questions in the margins may help you.

SYSTEMS

Not long ago the term 'system' was hardly used, but the idea of system has assumed more and more importance which is reflected in the widespread use of the term. We are surrounded by ecosystems, we create and live in political and social systems,

Part 5 APPLICATION OF READING STRATEGIES TO A PASSAGE CONCERNED WITH DEFINITIONS

[1] Is the brain a system, part of a system, or both?
[2] Why is it a problem word?

we use transport systems and indeed, the most important part of us is a vital and mysterious system, our brain, part of the central nervous system.[1] The word *systems*, however, is a problem word.[2] Although everyone knows (or thinks they know) what it means, it turns out to be surprisingly difficult to define precisely. Systems are commonly defined in the dictionary as 'a group of objects united by some form of interaction or interdependdence; an organic or organized whole such as the solar system or a new telegraph system'. This definition suggests that there are differences in the kinds of systems. The solar system is a natural system, a telegraph system is designed by man. There are also hybrid systems which are combinations of natural and man-made systems—hydroelectric plants, for example, or modern dairies.

1 List the different systems mentioned which are:
    a natural   b man-made   c hybrid.

The dictionary definition is a good introduction to a discussion of systems. However, it is not a sufficient explanation of a special meaning of the term. The special meaning of the term 'systems' emerged during and after World War II as a result of the need for building combat aircraft. In building such aircraft, designers realized that they could not simply take an existing airplane and add weapons, bomb and fuel storage space, communication and detection equipment, and protective armour. Adding such equipment at random restricted the plane's carrying capacity, speed, manoeuverability, range of flight, and other vital functions. What emerged from this realization[3] was a new method of planning and development in which designers learned that they first had to identify the purpose and performance expectations before they could develop all the parts that made up[4] the systems as a whole. It is the system as a whole—and not its parts separately—that must be planned, designed, installed, and managed. What

[3] What did they realize?

[4] In this context *make up* means:
a form
b invent
c reconcile
d decide.

Unit 4   DEFINITIONS

is really significant is not how the individual components function separately but the way they interact and are integrated into the system for the purpose of achieving the goal of the system. Generalizing from this example,[5] systems can be defined as deliberately designed synthetic organisms comprised of interrelated and interacting components which are employed to function in an integrated fashion to attain predetermined purposes.

[5] What example?

2   In what way did the need to build combat aircraft result in the new concept of systems?
3   What was new about the 'new method' mentioned?
4   What is important about the parts of a system?
5   Which of the systems mentioned in paragraph 1 does this definition exclude?

The concept of systems has rapidly expanded into new areas. Its military, industrial and business applications are enormous. Systems surround us everywhere. In the home, for example, there is a system whose purpose is to produce meals. The components of the system consist of the cook, the cooking equipment, the lighting, heating, water supply, storage and disposal facilities, the food, the dishes and the cookbook. All these interact in the performance of the processes which are necessary to accomplish the purpose of the system.[6] In the case of the example given, meal production, the components will interact in such processes as planning the meals, acquiring, storing, preserving and preparing food, as well as sanitation and environmental control. Systems thus have a purpose and it is the purpose which determines the components of the system and also the interrelation of the processes in which the components engage.[7] The purpose of any system is to produce a particular outcome. Systems can have different kinds of outcomes. To go back to the same example, the outcome of a meal-production system would be edible food.

[6] What interact in the performance of processes?

[7] What do the components and processes depend on?

Part 5   APPLICATION OF READING STRAGEGIES TO A PASSAGE CONCERNED WITH DEFINITIONS

6   This diagram illustrates the system described in the paragraph. Complete it with some of the specific information given.

PURPOSE	COMPONENTS	PROCESSES	OUTCOME
	storage facilities		

The planning, the acquisition of the food, the sanitation, and so on, can be viewed as subsystems that make up the meal-production system. A subsystem is a part of a total system which is designed to carry out a purpose[8] whose attainment is necessary in order to achieve the overall purpose of the system.[9] Subsystems operate in an integrated fashion. In a meal-production system, planning is integrated with and influenced by food acquisition, which then interacts with storage and preservation, preparation, and the other subsystems.[10] The effectiveness of the system depends on how well they interfunction.

From: Bela Banathy, *Systems and Education* in *Instructional Systems* Belmont, California (Fearon Publishers) 1968

[8] What is designed to carry out a purpose?

[9] What is necessary in order to achieve the purpose of the whole system?

[10] What interacts with storage etc.?

7   Underline the definition in the paragraph.

8   Use information from the paragraph to complete the following table.

Concept defined	Examples of concepts	Generalization about the behaviour of subsystems	Examples of behaviour	Importance of subsystem in relation to system

Unit 4 DEFINITIONS

WRITING A SUMMARY

Answer the following questions about the passage. Write your answers as complete statements so that they provide a summary of the passage.

1. How can we define the concept of 'systems'?
2. What does a system consist of?
3. What determines the content of a system?
4. What is a subsystem?
5. In what areas does the concept of systems have applications?

Unit 5 Classifications

Preview
This unit is concerned with the ways in which passages organize information in the form of classifications.

Part 1
draws attention to the purpose of classifications and how they are used in communication.

Part 2
deals with different types of classifications.

Part 3
practises ways of expressing classifications.

Part 4
shows the ways in which simple classifications can be expanded in passages.

Part 5
provides practice in applying reading strategies to a passage concerned with classifications.

Unit 5   CLASSIFICATIONS

**Part 1
The purpose of classifications**

The first scientists to arrive on Planet Zeta found a wide variety of plant life. Consequently, they had to consider the problem of how to classify the different plants. Read the following descriptions of some of the plants they found and then answer the questions.

PLANT A
Travels large distances by moving on its roots.
Catches and eats other plants.
Produces a high-pitched whistle.

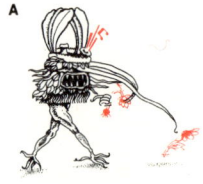

PLANT B
Does not move.
Converts crude petroleum to food.
Silent.
Emits a pale yellow light in the dark.

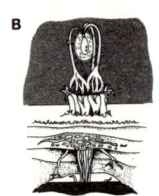

PLANT C
Roots grow upwards and fix it to other plants.
Traps and eats insects.
When approached, flashes a bright red light.

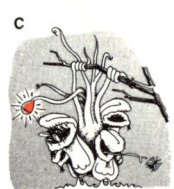

PLANT D
Roots grow upwards and enable it to move from tree to tree.
Lives in colonies.
Cultivates plants and insects for food.
Emits heat at regular intervals.

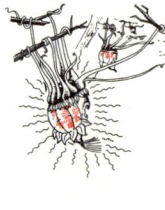

The descriptions give us information about the following characteristics:

direction in which the roots grow
movement
food
production of sound, light or heat.

1   What characteristics do the following plants have in common?

a A and D   b B and C   c A and B

Part 1   THE PURPOSE OF CLASSIFICATIONS

2   In what respects do the following plants differ?
    a   A and B
    b   C and D

3   Which plants are similar with respect to:
the direction in which the roots grow
the food they eat
movement?

4   We can classify the plants using the characteristics included in the description as criteria. Complete the following diagram which classifies the plants according to their ability to move.

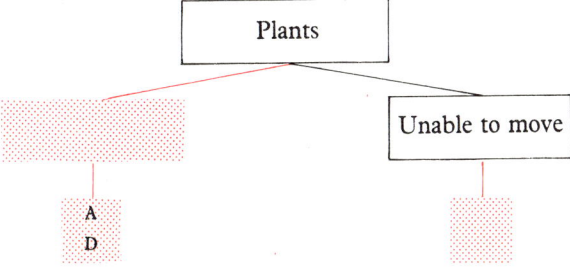

A classification includes the following information:

Entity: e.g. plants
Criteria: e.g. ability to move
Groups: e.g. those which can move;
            those which cannot move
Examples: e.g. plants A and D
              plants B and C

Here is one way of classifying the plants on Planet Zeta:

Plants can be classified according to their ability to move. The first group consists of those plants which use their roots to move. The second group consists of plants which are unable to move. Examples of the former are plants A and D. Examples of the latter are plants B and C.

Unit 5 CLASSIFICATIONS

5   Complete the following diagram to show the classification of plants on Zeta according to whether they produce sound, light or heat.

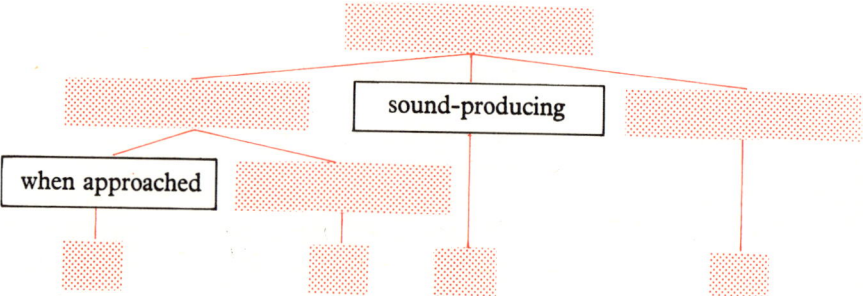

This type of diagram is called a *tree diagram*. Here, it is used to show how we can divide groups into sub-groups.

Part 2
Types of classifications

Activity 1

There are two main ways in which classifications can be organized. Each of the following passages shows a different way of organizing a classification. Read the first passage in order to complete the diagrams after it, then answer question 1.

PROBLEMS OF CLASSIFYING MICRO-ORGANISMS
Micro-organisms were once regarded as being members of the plant kingdom, apart from protozoa which were classed as animals. It became obvious that this arbitrary classification resulted in confusions, even absurdities. A virus infecting an animal cannot, by any criterion, be termed a plant. There became almost as many systems of classification as there were microbiologists. In order to clarify the nature of micro-organisms, we may distinguish between those, like fungi and some algae, which have a cell structure similar to higher organisms and those, like the bacteria and the blue-green algae, which have a comparatively simple cell structure. We will refer to the former as 'higher protists' and to the latter as 'lower protists'. Both

these groups are placed in the kingdom Protista. The viruses and the recently described subviral agents cannot at present be adequately classified, so we shall place them in a group of their own.
From: Gerald Wasky *Teach Yourself Microbiology* (Hodder and Stoughton)

Complete diagram 1 to show the traditional classification of micro-organisms.

DIAGRAM 1

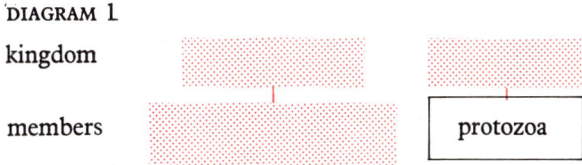

Now complete diagram 2 to show the system of classification used by the writer.

DIAGRAM 2

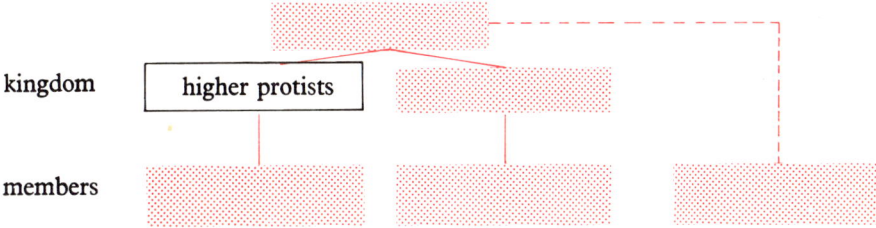

1   Why was the traditional classification inadequate?

Now read the second passage in order to complete the diagram after it.

CHORDATES
The chordates are a large and highly diverse animal group which comprises vertebrates or animals with backbones (often referred to as the higher chordates) as well as a group of animals which lack vertebrae but which resemble vertebrates in other important respects. These are referred to as protochordates, or lower chordates. The vertebrates are divided into five classes: fishes, amphibians, reptiles, birds and mammals. Each of these five classes can be further subdivided into smaller groups: for example, mammals can be classified into 18 groups,

Unit 5 CLASSIFICATIONS

known as orders. Examples of orders are marsupials (such as kangaroos), primates (including man and the monkeys), and carnivores (including dogs and cats). The class of reptiles consists of five orders: examples of these are crocodilians (including crocodiles and alligators) and squamata, examples of which are snakes and lizards.

From: *Larousse Encyclopedia of Animal Life* (Hamlyn)

Now complete diagram 3 to show the classification made in the above paragraph.

DIAGRAM 3

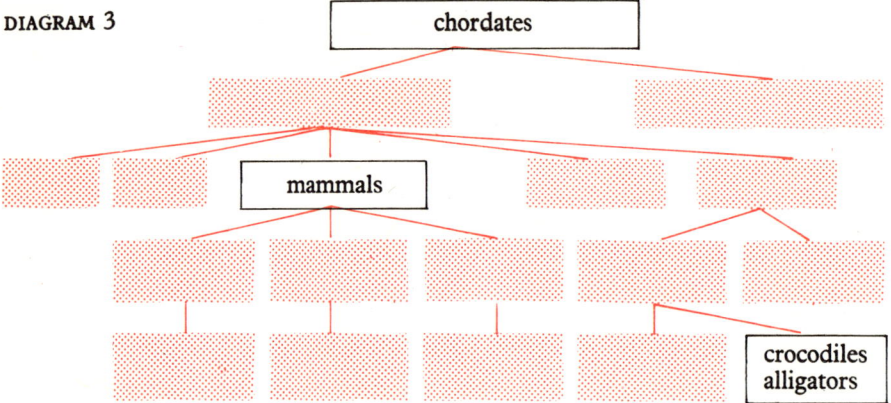

In the first passage (on micro-organisms) the writer is concerned to place organisms into groups to which they belong. The writer proceeds from the specific to the general.

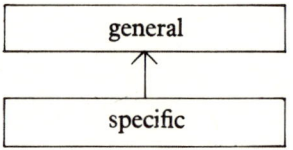

In the second passage the writer is concerned to divide a general group into smaller groups and give specific examples of those groups. He procedes from the general to the specific.

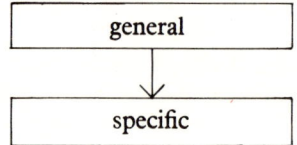

Part 2 TYPES OF CLASSIFICATIONS

Underline one sentence in the first passage which expresses the member/class relationship. Identify the member and its corresponding class.

Underline one sentence in the second passage which expresses the class/member relationship. Identify the class and its corresponding members. Complete the following table with markers of the two types of classification that are found in the two passages.

TYPE 1

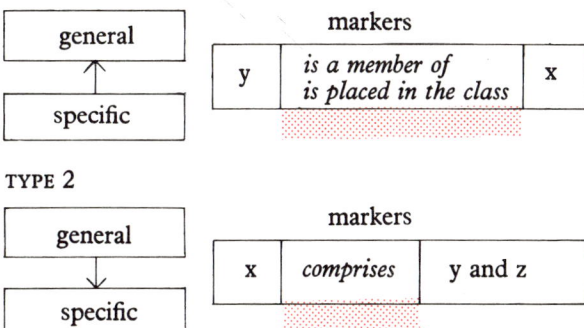

TYPE 2

general	markers		
↓	x	comprises	y and z
specific			

Activity 2

This activity shows how a writer expresses similarities and differences, on the basis of which a classification is made. Study the passage and decide which of the two types the classification belongs to.

TYPES OF GOODS AND SERVICES
In order to understand economic behaviour we need to refer to specific goods and services. For example, when analysing consumer expenditure and household decision-making, it is convenient to classify commodities in such types as: food, clothing, alcoholic drink and tobacco, durable household goods, vehicles, etc. However, this classification is less helpful when looked at from the point of view of the production of goods.

Consider the basis on which this classification for household decision-making rests. In analysing consumer expenditure we employed as a criterion the use to which a commodity is put. So we allocated all expenditure aimed at purchasing something for people to wear to a category called clothing. But in a sense, the notion of use is

Unit 5 CLASSIFICATIONS

completely arbitrary. Why did we not group products together according to colour, size, shape, or weight, for example? Red cheeses have a common characteristic with red hats. Cars and elephants resemble each other more closely in weight than do cars and bicycles, and there are other criteria which could form the basis for quite different subdivisions of items. The reason for basing our analysis on use is that it helps us to understand the reasons for consumer behaviour. When deciding whether to buy a ballpoint pen or a pencil we tend to think of these items as having very similar uses.

Consider now the business as a decision-making unit. In some cases the criterion of use is still helpful. For example, if we wish to understand the behaviour of retail shops our use criterion will still be appropriate. Shops are commonly organized for the sale of goods used for the same general purposes. There are food stores, clothing shops, sweet shops, pet shops, etc. But insofar as the business of production is concerned, we find that a wide range of business behaviour is not so much use-oriented as process-oriented. It is common to find firms which are skilled in a particular production process, but whose products cover a wide range of different uses. A task like the welding of steel tubes, for example, can be relatively easily adapted to the production of chair frames or car roof racks as well as of many other things. The processes of spinning and weaving natural fibres into cloths are much the same whether the material is to be used for clothing, furnishings or sails for fishing boats. This underlines the point that the relevant criterion for classifying goods must be an operationally useful one. In other words, it must tell us something of the basis on which decisions are made.

Adapted from: C. D. Harbury: *An Introduction to Economic Behaviour* (Fontana) 1971.

Now answer these questions about the basis on which this type of classification is made.

Part 2 TYPES OF CLASSIFICATIONS

1 What criteria are used for classifying commodities

a for household decision-making?
b for businesses concerned with production?
c for other types of businesses?

2 Why is use chosen as a criterion for classifying products?

3 What determines the choice of criteria for classifying goods?

4 In what respect are cars and elephants similar?

5 Complete the table to show how the same process can be employed for products with different uses.

PRODUCT   USES   PROCESS

steel tubes

spinning and weaving

Activity 3

Expressing the two types of classifications
Write a short paragraph based on each of the following diagrams. Use the expressions you identified in Activity 1.

TYPE 1

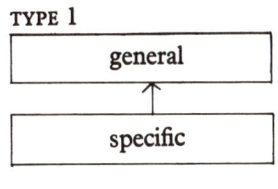

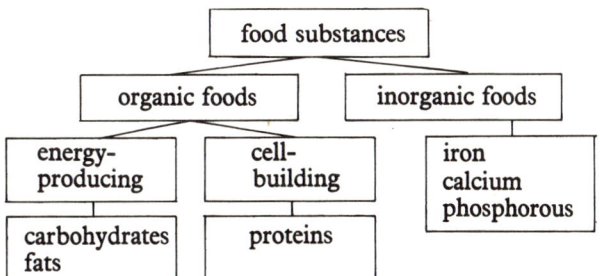

Unit 5 CLASSIFICATIONS

TYPE 2

```
general
   ↓
specific
```

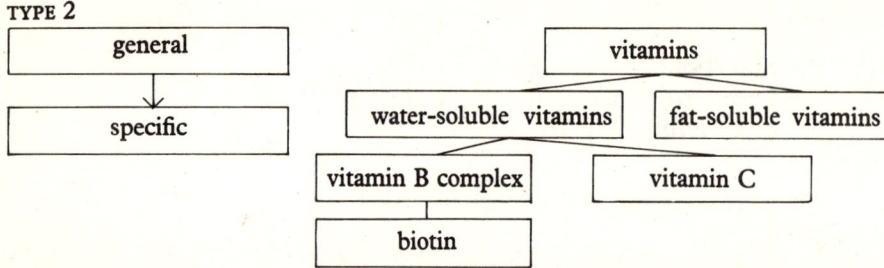

Part 3
Ways of expressing classifications

In Part 2 attention was drawn to the two types of classifications and to the way classifications are based on a system of similarities and differences. In this part we will practise ways of expressing the two types of classifications. We will also study expressions which indicate the criteria used in classifications.

Activity 4

Ways of expressing criteria
Read the following paragraph and underline the criteria used for classification.

Example: Before Mendeleev, chemical elements were classified according to <u>their properties</u>.

Before Mendeleev, chemical elements were classified according to their properties. Mendeleev's contribution was to find a much more exact system of classification, based on atomic weight. More recently, the basis of classification has moved to atomic number. Thus chemical classification has a quantitative basis while biological classification only has a qualitative basis. The basic criteria considered in biological classification are anatomical, ecological and genetical facts relating to each species. Sometimes it is also convenient to group animals with respect to their behaviour—their feeding habits, for example. The point about biological classification is that, unlike a quantitative classification, it gives few grounds for predicting the occurrence of unrecognized species.

You should have underlined the criteria used in the following classifications:

Part 3 WAYS OF EXPRESSING CLASSIFICATIONS

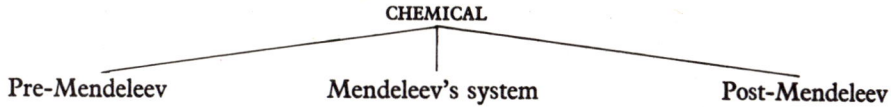

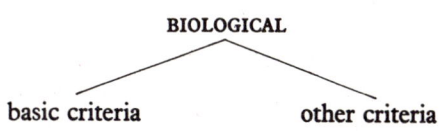

Now underline the markers which indicate that the writer is referring to criteria.

Example: Before Mendeleev, chemical elements were classified <u>according to</u> their properties.

Now use the markers you found in the paragraph to complete the following table:

	markers	criteria
x can be classified	*according to*	y

Activity 5

Read the following statements and rewrite them so as to express the criteria used. Include the patterns you identified in Activity 4.

Example: Speech sounds may be divided into two types: those in which the air stream from the lungs is impeded and those in which the air stream is not impeded. (*articulation*)
Speech sounds may be divided into two types according to their articulation.

1   Speech sounds may be classified into those which are central in the syllable and those which are marginal. (*the place in the syllable*)
2   Consonants can be subdivided into such groups as bilabials, dentals, alveolars, etc. (*the place of articulation*)
3   Consonants can be classed into such groups as plosives, affricates and nasals. (*the manner of articulation*)

Unit 5 CLASSIFICATIONS

4   Vowel sounds can be separated into back, central and front vowels. (*the part of the tongue which is raised*)

5   Vowel sounds can be divided into such groups as close and open. (*the degree to which the tongue is raised*)

**Part 4
Expanded
classifications**

Part 3 practised different ways of expressing classifications and the criteria used in making them. This part studies how a classification can be combined in a passage; for example with definitions, descriptions, and exemplification.

Activity 6

Study the following passage and answer the questions which follow it.

MUSICAL INSTRUMENTS
Most authorities divide musical instruments into four major classes according to the principles of acoustics. These are: idiophones, membranophones, aerophones (wind instruments) and cordophones (stringed instruments).

Idiophones are instruments made of materials which are inherently resonant. That is, they produce sounds by themselves. They can be subdivided according to the method by which they are made to vibrate: by percussion, by bending flexible material, or by friction. One of the most common examples of the first group is the marimba.

Membranophones are instruments which produce sounds by means of the vibration of a tight membrane. The best examples of these are drums.

Aerophones must have two essentials: a body enclosing a column of air and a device for interrupting the air flow. The latter may be the edge of the instrument (as in flutes), or the player's lips (as in a trumpet); or it may be the movement of a reed (as in a clarinet). The nature of this device determines the major groups of wind instruments.

Cordophones emit sound by means of the vibration of a tightly-stretched string. Cordophones

Part 4 EXPANDED CLASSIFICATIONS

are usually divided into classes according to whether the vibrations are made by plucking, by striking or by friction. Examples of each class are: the guitar, the piano and the violin.

Adapted (slightly simplified) from Jean Jenkins: *Musical Instruments Handbook* Horniman Museum (GLC/ILEA)

1   Complete the following statements to show the criteria used.

Musical instruments are classified on the basis of ……

Idiophones can be classified according to how ……

Aerophones are subdivided according to the …… of the device for ……

Cordophones are subdivided according to the …… by which they ……

2   Complete the following diagram to show the classification made in the passage.

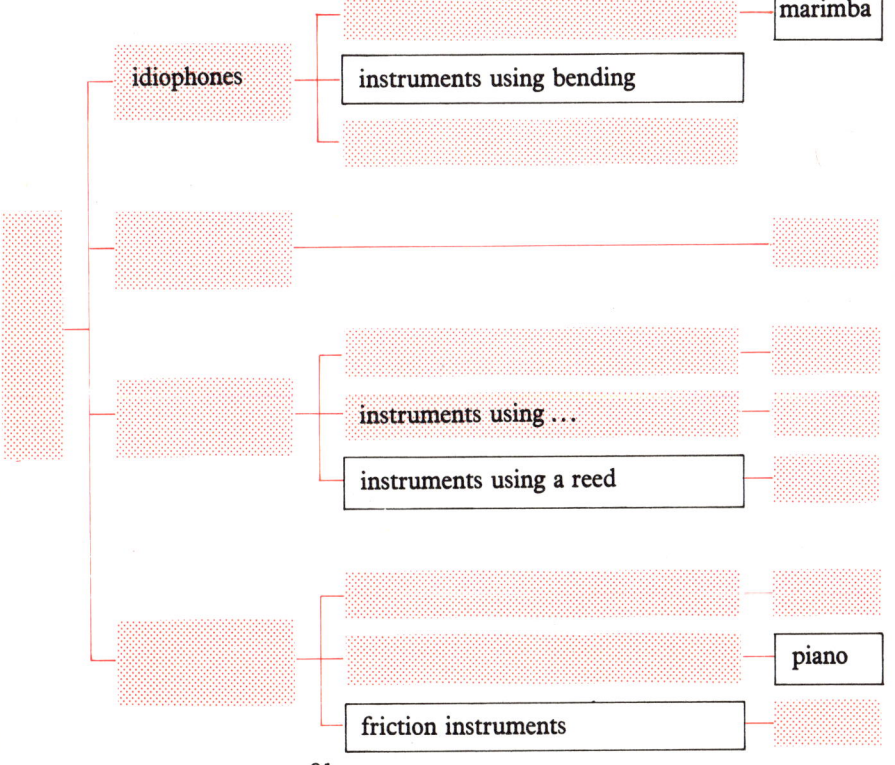

Unit 5 CLASSIFICATIONS

3   Two of the classes of instruments are defined in the passage, using the structure:
concept = class + characteristics. Underline these two definitions. Use the generalizations made about the other two groups to write a similar definition for each.

Activity 7

Study the following paragraph and then complete the diagram after it.

CLASSIFICATION OF PLASTICS
The behaviour of plastics when heated provides the basis for the distinction between the two main classes of plastics available today. Those like polythene, PVC, perspex and nylon, which soften when heated and become rigid when cooled again, are called thermoplastics; with further heating and cooling these plastics can be made to change their shape repeatedly—like the gramophone record. This processing is possible because only weak bonding is present between neighbouring molecules, and when warm the molecules slide very easily past one another. On the other hand, plastics which become rigid on further heating and cannot be softened again are called thermosetting plastics. Examples are Bakelite and Melamine. These materials consist of polymer chains which react with one another at points of contact so that they become strongly linked together in three dimensions. The intermolecular bonds then prevent relative movement of the original chains—in fact the material is really one single molecule.
From: C. W. A. Newey *The Plastics and Steel Industries* in *The Man Made World* (Open University)—slightly shortened

Plastics

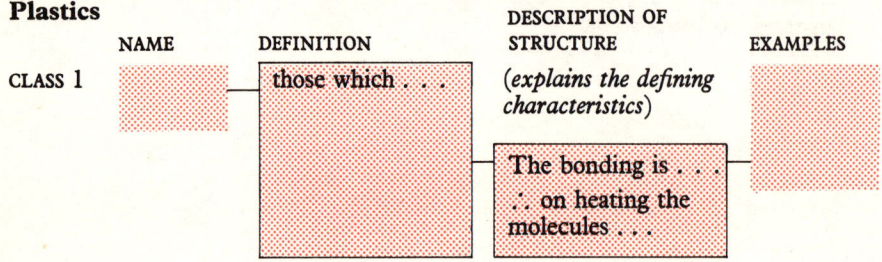

Part 5 APPLICATION OF READING STRATEGIES TO A PASSAGE CONCERNED WITH CLASSIFICATIONS

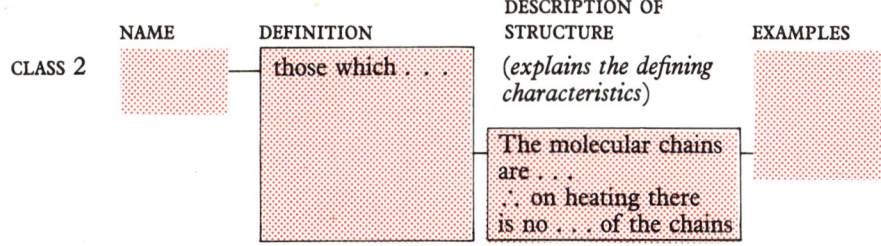

The diagram you have completed shows the structure of the information in the paragraph.

**Part 5
Application of reading strategies**

We are now going to study a passage which is concerned with classification. The passage is about learning, theories of learning and their implications. First look at the pictures and answer the questions about them. Your answer will help you predict some of the content of the passage.

1   In what ways are the two learning situations different with respect to:
    a   the nature of the learner
    b   the nature of the learning task
    c   where the learning takes place?
2   Which of the following statements is true for both situations?
    a   Learning is the acquisition of knowledge by study.
    b   Learning changes the learner in some way.
    c   Learning involves a spontaneous physiological response.

Now read as much of the passage as is necessary in order to find:
a   a definition of learning which is applicable to all types of learning
b   an example of reward training

Unit 5 CLASSIFICATIONS

    c   examples of how punishment is used in every-day life

    d   the difference between the two major approaches to learning.

Now read the passage carefully paragraph by paragraph in order to answer the comprehension questions.

THE PSYCHOLOGY OF LEARNING
What is learning?

People are continually engaged in some learning activity or other—learning to ride a bicycle or speak a foreign language, to dance, swim, play a card-game, handle a pneumatic drill, manage a shop or administer a government department. How is it that we can use the word 'learning' about such a varied set of activities? The only similarity[1] lies in the fact that in each case there is a change in the learner brought about[2] in some way by the interaction of the environment with the individual. If we adopt as a provisional definition of an instance of learning 'any more or less permanent change of behaviour which is the result of experience' we find that even the most primitive animals are capable of some learning. In fact, in a very special sense, it can also be said that plants are able to learn.

[1] Similarity between what?

[2] In this context *bring about* means:
a   bring approximately
b   attract
c   cause to happen.

1   What is the justification for the writer's statement that 'plants are able to learn'?

Theories of learning

So far we have emphasized that a great variety of learning activities have much in common. It would, however, be a mistake to underestimate the differences between the types of learning involved in a rat finding its way out of a maze and a university student solving a problem in nuclear physics.[3] There are two extreme approaches to this diversity of learning. One is to regard the 'higher mental processes' as merely a complex form of animal stimulus-response learning. At the other extreme is the position that S-R learning is a curious

[3] Does *underestimate* something mean to give too much or too little importance to something?
∴ *it would be a mistake to underestimate the differences* means that the differences are/are not important.

Part 5 APPLICATION OF READING STRATEGIES TO A PASSAGE CONCERNED WITH CLASSIFICATIONS

laboratory phenomenon appropriate to an explanation of some animal learning but of no relevance to the process of human learning.

2 What two extreme forms of learning are mentioned?

3 What other kinds of approaches are implied?

Behaviourist or Stimulus-Response theories have been extremely influential. The simplest type of S-R learning is usually described under the heading 'conditioning'. It is convenient to separate conditioning into two broad classes: classical and instrumental conditioning. The essential operation in classical conditioning is the pairing[4] of two stimuli, as a result of which the first stimulus elicits the response previously elicited by the second.[5] The Pavlovian experiment in which dogs learned to salivate to the sound of a bell which had been paired repeatedly with food presentations has been taken to be the prototype of classical conditioning.[6] Instrumental conditioning (or operant conditioning) is an experimental procedure in which an animal is given reinforcement after it spontaneously makes a particular response, and the intensity of the response then increases.[7] Instrumental conditioning experiments can be classified according to the type of reinforcement into those using rewards and those using punishments. Both reward training and omission training use rewards. The former type of experiment is illustrated by the famous 'Skinner box'. There are two main kinds of experiments using punishment: escape training and avoidance conditioning. The latter can be subdivided into passive and active avoidance[8]. In avoidance conditioning the animal is given, for example, a mild[9] electric shock. Then a warning signal such as a red light is given, which enables the animal to avoid the shock. In active avoidance the animal makes a specific response, such as going into a different compartment in order to avoid the shock. In passive avoidance the animal must learn not to go into the compartment where there are shocks.

[5] What is the consequence of the pairing of the stimuli?

[7] Why does the intensity of the response increase?

[8] What can be subdivided into passive and active avoidance?

[4] In this context *pairing* means:
a association
b dividing into twos
c classifying.

[6] What is the prototype of classical conditioning?

[9] In this context *mild* means:
a pleasant
b warm
c not bitter
d not strong.

4   Complete the following diagram showing the classification made in the paragraph.

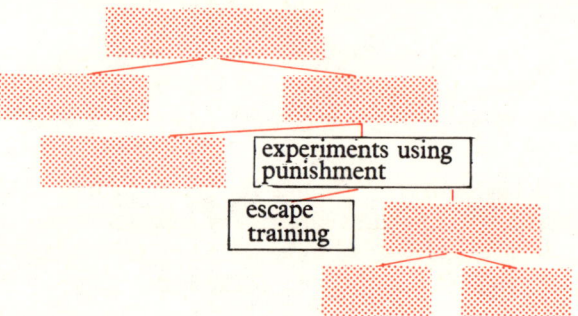

5   What criterion is used to classify instrumental conditioning experiments?

6   Underline the definition given of instrumental conditioning.

7   What is the essential difference between active and passive avoidance?

Implications of learning theories
It is apparent that conditioning is relevant for many social and educational questions. The Skinnerian theories led straight, for example, to the development of programmed learning and teaching machines. The use of punishment to change behaviour has even profounder implications. In everyday life punishment is widely used to prevent or eliminate undesirable behaviour. Parents introduce it in various ways in bringing up their children;[10] society uses it in the fight against crime.

Other implications for education are suggested by the findings of psychologists who do not accept behaviourist (S-R) theories. Some psychologists, for example, have maintained that language-learning is essentially a process of cognitive organization and rule-formation, not a repetition of Stimulus-Response associations. Another theory is that put forward[11] by Harry Harlow that organisms learn to learn by eliminating erroneous behaviour. The 'learning to learn' philosophy is behind a good many developments in present-day curricula,[12] where the emphasis is put not on the knowledge

[10]
What do parents use?

[11]
Put forward a theory means:
a   propose
b   postpone
c   verify.

[12]
This means that present-day curricula are
a   more developed than
b   based on
c   more up to date than
the 'learning to learn' philosophy.

Part 5 APPLICATION OF READING STRATEGIES TO A PASSAGE CONCERNED WITH CLASSIFICATIONS

to be acquired by the learner but on the learning strategies that he must develop. Lastly, the tendency today is to regard the learner as an individual with his own rate and strategies for learning and not as a human pigeon manipulated by an impersonal experimenter.

8   Do the examples show that conditioning is or is not relevant for society and education?
∴ *apparent* means:
    a   superficial
    b   clear
    c   not real.

9   Complete the following table:

Learning theory	Educational implications

WRITING A SUMMARY
Answer the following questions on the passage. Write your answers as complete statements so that they provide a summary of the passage.

1   How can we define learning?
2   What are the two main approaches to learning?
3   What are the two main types of conditioning?
4   What is the essential operation in each type of conditioning?
5   What is an example of a non-behaviourist theory?
6   What is an implication of this theory for education?

Unit 6 Hypotheses

Preview

This unit is concerned with passages involving the formulation and investigation of hypotheses. It also provides a review of the concepts studied in other units (generalization, description, definition, and classification) and shows how these methods of organizing information are used in academic investigations.

Part 1

draws attention to the nature of hypotheses and their place in investigations.

Part 2

deals with passages containing hypotheses and evidence.

Part 3

is concerned with the use of hypotheses to solve problems.

Part 4

practises ways of expressing hypotheses.

Part 5

gives practice in applying reading strategies to a passage which reports an investigation.

Part 1
The nature of hypotheses

Read the following account of a crime and answer the questions.

THE SITUATION

A man was found dead in a hotel bedroom at 4 p.m. one Saturday afternoon. Four people were near the scene of the crime about this time:

Colonel Crab, who found the body.
Mary Fish, who was in the next bedroom.
Tony Plum and Professor Peach, who were in the corridors.

Their positions are marked on this plan:

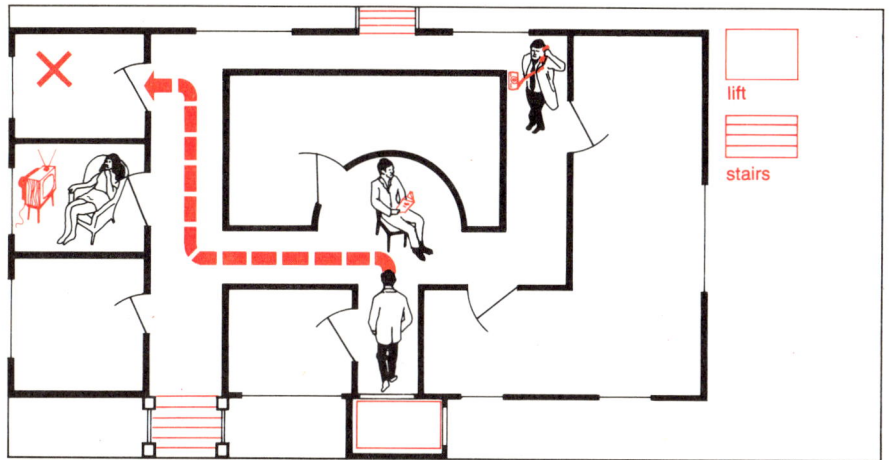

THE EVIDENCE

Mary Fish said she was watching television the whole time and heard nothing. She was able to give accurate details of the film she was watching.

Tony Plum said he was reading a detective story in the corridor from 3 p.m. until the police arrived. He said he did not move and did not see anyone go past.

Professor Peach said he was taking a long-distance phone-call between 3:45 and 4:05 and saw no one go past. The telephone operator confirmed the length of his call.

Unit 6 HYPOTHESES

Colonel Crab said he got out of the lift at 3:55 and went straight to Mr. X's room. He said that there was no one sitting in the corridor at this time.

THE HYPOTHESES
Detective Inspector Apple considered the following hypotheses:

Hypothesis 1 Mary Fish committed the crime.
What is the evidence against this?

Hypothesis 2 Tony Plum was the murderer.
What evidence is there for this?

Hypothesis 3 Professor Peach committed the murder.
Does the evidence support this hypothesis?

Hypothesis 4 Colonel Crab murdered Mr. X.
Does Tony Plum's evidence support this hypothesis?

THE INVESTIGATION
Detective Inspector Apple started by making deductions from some of the hypotheses. He considered the following questions:

If Colonel Crab's story was correct, was Tony Plum telling the truth?
If Tony Plum was telling the truth, why didn't he see Colonel Crab?

The Inspector then collected further evidence. The manager of the hotel told him that Colonel Crab was a well-known and respected businessman and that Tony Plum owed the hotel a large amount of money. A porter said that he saw Plum looking worried and nervous after lunch. The detective also interviewed a lift technician who had called to repair the hotel lifts which had not been working that day. He also interviewed the maid who had cleaned Mr. X's room that morning. The evidence convinced the Inspector that one of the suspects was lying and the Inspector concluded that this suspect was guilty.

Part 2 HYPOTHESES AND EVIDENCE

What did the Inspector conclude and what was his evidence?

There are many similarities between a police investigation and scientific methods of research. Both start from a problem. In both, hypotheses are important. As can be seen from this investigation, hypotheses are provisional explanations which are based on observation and can be tested by further observation. We can show this process as follows:

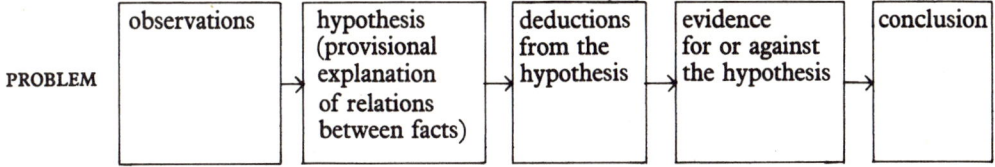

**Part 2
Hypotheses
and evidence**

We saw in Part 1 that hypotheses are based on observation and can be verified by evidence from further observations. The following passage concerns hypotheses and evidence for them. Read the passage in order to find the main hypothesis about how the earth is changing.

THE CHANGING EARTH
The last decade has brought about a revolution in our understanding of the earth and the forces that shape it. Centuries ago geographers noticed that the continents of Africa and South America appear to fit together like a jig-saw puzzle. In 1620 Sir Francis Bacon speculated that their similarity of shorelines could not be an accident though he did not consider actual movement. During the 1800s there were discoveries of identical fossils and rock layers in the two continents. In 1912 the German meteorologist Wegener put forward the hypothesis that all the continents of the earth have moved, on the grounds that they all seem to fit together like a jig-saw puzzle and that there are many similarities in the distribution of animals and plants. In his book *The Origin of Continents and Oceans* he wrote: 'The continents must have shifted. South America must have lain alongside Africa and the two parts must then have become

Unit 6 HYPOTHESES

increasingly separated over millions of years.' (See Figure 1.) Moreover, he suggested that the movement was the result of forces related to the spin of the earth.

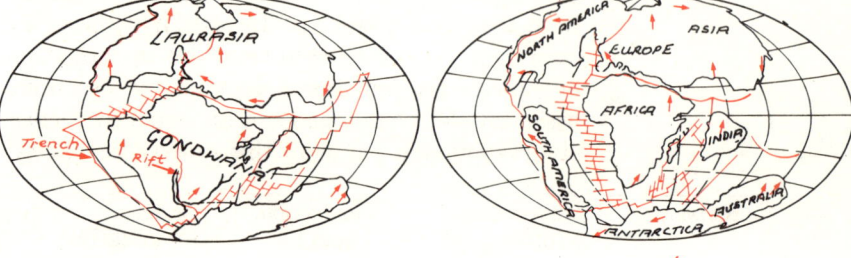

FIGURE 1

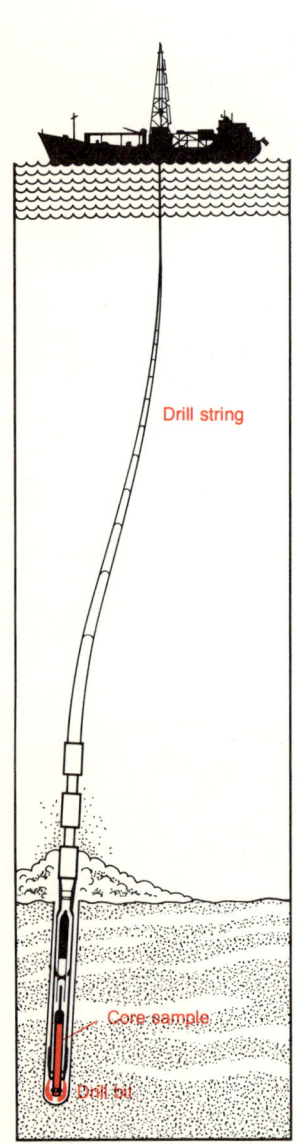

FIGURE 2

Wegener's idea was attacked for over half a century by the more conservative geologists who could not believe how continents could move, but now the evidence is becoming overwhelming that they do. Many earth scientists believe that the continents have moved apart and are continuing to move. The evidence comes from two quite different sources. One was the exploration of the geology of the oceans. The great advances in physical oceanography—including the use of drilling techniques to obtain rock and mud samples from the ocean floor—have revealed an unsuspected pattern (see Figure 2). There is, it appears, a system of rifts, like thin deep valleys running down the middle of all the oceans and round the continent of Antarctica. These rifts are steadily opening—the Atlantic Ocean was shown to be opening at a rate of 1 to 2 inches a year and parts of the Pacific floor, particularly off South America's west coast, are moving at four times this speed.

Other evidence comes from the study of paleo-geomagnetism. Rock layers keep permanently the direction of magnetic force that they had when they were formed in past geologic ages. It has been found that rocks in different continents can be matched according to their pole positions and this can be explained only by assuming that the continents have moved. It is thus possible to deduce that India was once near the South Pole and that much of Britain was in the arid desert zone near

Part 2 HYPOTHESES AND EVIDENCE

the equator. The Sahara, too, must have been at the South Pole, even though it is now 8000 miles away.

Based on these findings, some earth scientists have predicted that within the next 60 million years Central America will disappear, the Atlantic and Pacific will meet, Australia will be close to China and East Africa will have broken from the rest of the African continent. This new view of the earth certainly demonstrates the truth of the ancient Chinese belief that the one constant certainty in the world is change.

Adapted from: Samuel W. Matthews, *National Geographic Magazine* January 1973.

1   Complete the following table to summarize paragraph 1.

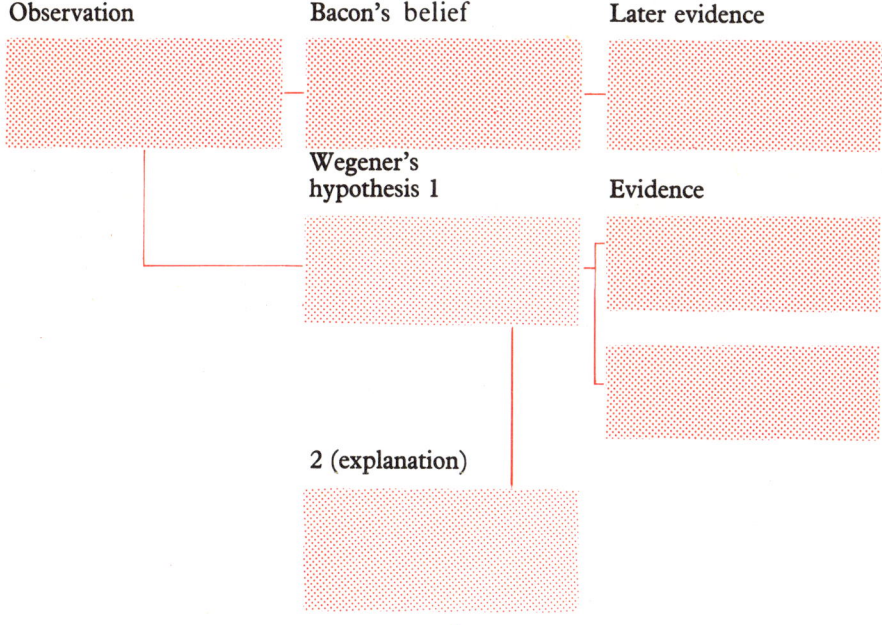

2   What evidence has oceanography provided and how was it obtained?

3   What other evidence supports the main hypothesis and how was it obtained?

Unit 6 HYPOTHESES

4   Which of the following maps shows the predicted position of the continents in 60 million years' time?

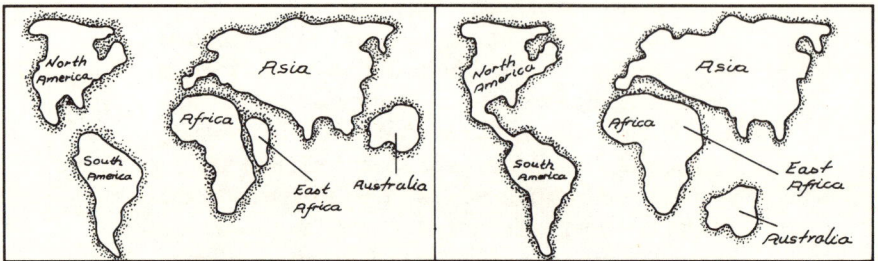

**Part 3
Hypotheses
in solving problems**

We saw in Part 2 how hypotheses can be tested by evidence. This part concerns the use of hypotheses to reach conclusions when solving problems.

Activity 1

Read this problem and its solution which are taken from the end of a chapter on hormones in a textbook.

QUESTION
Young rats may be retarded in growth either as a result of deficiency of thyroxin or deficiency of a hormone S secreted by the pituitary gland. In a few sentences, suggest how a biologist could determine whether a group of rats showing retardation of growth were deficient in thyroxin or in hormone S.

1   What is known about retardation of growth in rats?
2   What problem does the biologist have to solve?

ANSWER
There are two approaches. First, to produce normal growth in the group of deficient rats by making good the deficiency. If giving them thyroxin leads to normal growth, then they were probably deficient in thyroxin. If giving them hormone S leads to normal growth, they were probably deficient in hormone S.
    The second approach is to operate on normal rats in such a way as to produce the same pattern of retarded growth. If removing the thyroid glands

Part 3 HYPOTHESES IN SOLVING PROBLEMS

leads to this type of retarded growth, the original rats were probably suffering from deficiency in thyroxin. If removing the pituitary leads to retarded growth, then the group of retarded rats were probably suffering from deficiency of hormone S.

A final experiment should now be done. In this the operated rats are given either thyroxin or hormone S as appropriate. Assuming that this leads to normal growth, there will be strong confirmation that the conclusions from the results of the operation are correct.

Adapted from: Open University Science Foundation Course Unit 18 *Cells and Organisms*

3   What is the difference between the two approaches? What procedure do they have in common?

4   Complete the following table to show the hypotheses and their corresponding conclusions in each approach.

	HYPOTHESES	CONCLUSIONS
Approach 1	Giving the rats thyroxin leads to normal growth.	
Approach 2		
		The conclusions from the results of the operation will be confirmed.

Activity 2   Read the following problem and answer the questions after it.

Unit 6 HYPOTHESES

A farmer has to cross a river one day with a dog, a sheep and some hay. The only boat he has is so small that he can only get one animal or the hay into it besides himself. The farmer knows that the dog is liable to attack sheep and that the sheep cannot resist eating hay. How does the farmer manage to get himself, the animals and the hay across the river safely?

1   First hypothesis: the farmer takes the hay, leaving the dog and the sheep together. What will be the consequence?
2   Second hypothesis: the farmer takes the dog, leaving the sheep and the hay. What consequence can you deduce?
3   What must the farmer take first?
4   Draw a diagram to show the position of the farmer, the dog, the sheep and the hay when the farmer returns from the first journey.
5   The farmer now has several alternatives. They are expressed in the following hypotheses. Choose the hypothesis which expresses the correct alternative.
   a   The farmer takes the dog and goes back for the hay.
   b   The farmer takes the hay and then goes back for the dog.
   c   The farmer takes the dog, returns with the sheep, leaves the sheep and takes the hay.
   d   The farmer takes either the dog or the hay, leaves it on the other side and returns for the other.
6   How many times does the farmer have to cross the river?

Part 4
Ways of expressing hypotheses

We saw in Part 1 that a hypothesis expresses a relation between circumstances. Read the following hypothesis:

If retarded rats are given thyroxin, their growth will be normal.

The hypothesis expresses a relation between two

Part 4 WAYS OF EXPRESSING HYPOTHESES

circumstances. It indicates that normal growth (circumstance B) depends on giving the rats thyroxin (circumstance A).

Activity 3

Look at the following statements and answer the questions after them.

1   Rainbows can be seen only if the observer is between the sun and the rain, and if the sun is not too high.

> On what circumstances does seeing a rainbow depend?
> The observer must be ......
> The sun ......

2   A rainbow is formed when light from the sun is dispersed by drops of water.

> What circumstances are necessary for a rainbow to be formed?
> It is necessary for ...... to ......

3   An observer will not see a rainbow unless there are drops of water suspended in the air.

> What depends on the presence of drops of water in the air?

Activity 4

This activity practises ways of expressing the dependence of one set of circumstances on another.

1   Read the following description of an eclipse of the sun and label the diagram.

When the moon comes between the earth and the sun, there is an eclipse of the sun. However, an observer will not see a total eclipse unless he is in the region marked B. In this region no light at all is received from the sun. If you are in regions A or C, you will receive light from part of the sun but not from all of it. In these regions a partial eclipse is seen.

2   Now answer these questions about the passage.

Unit 6 HYPOTHESES

a In what circumstances is there an eclipse of the sun?
b In what circumstances do you see
   —a total eclipse
   —a partial eclipse?

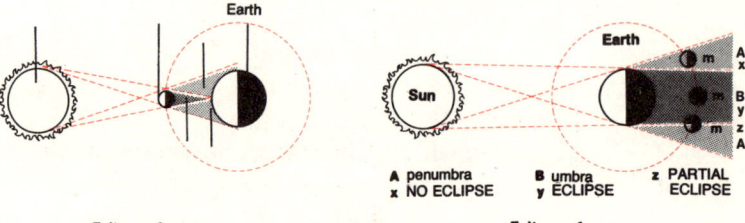

Eclipse of sun   Eclipse of moon

3 Use the diagram to complete the following description of eclipses of the moon.

When ...... light from the sun cannot reach the moon. If this happens, there is .... There will not be a total eclipse ...... the moon lies in the umbra. If the moon lies in the penumbra ...... since the moon merely becomes less bright. ......, it is partially eclipsed.

We saw in Part 3 that hypotheses serve as a basis for deductions—that is, we can predict consequences from them. For example,

If the farmer leaves the dog with the sheep   (hypothesis)

the dog will attack the sheep.   (predicted consequence)

In the above example the dog's attack (circumstance B) is the consequence which is predicted from leaving the dog with the sheep (circumstance A).

Activity 5

This activity practises ways of predicting the consequences of a set of circumstances. The following passage mentions the importation of a specific foreign species of animal. Read the passage to find out the predicted consequences of this importation.

Part 4   WAYS OF EXPRESSING HYPOTHESES

The survival of an exotic species in a new habitat depends on many factors—chiefly, of course, the availability of food and the presence or absence of predators and parasites. If food is too scarce or food-getting too competitive, or if predators are too numerous, the exotic species will not survive. If food is abundant and predators are absent, it will rapidly multiply to plague proportions and disrupt the life of every organism (including man) in the habitat. Even if the balance between food and predators is just right, the species may produce important secondary ecological consequences. A good example of how an imported species can affect an ecosystem is the introduction of the horse into North America by Spanish explorers in the 15th century. Many of these animals escaped, and they bred and prospered in the wild. Later, they were domesticated by the Plains Indians, and the culture of these bison-hunting people was profoundly altered by the greater mobility conferred upon them by the horse.

Taken from: *Man, Nature and Ecology,* © 1974 Aldus Books, London

1   The relationship between the two main factors mentioned allows the formulation of three alternatives. Complete the table to show each alternative and its predicted consequence.

	Alternative 1	*Alternative 2*	*Alternative 3*
Given situation	a b c		
Predicted consequence			

Unit 6   HYPOTHESES

2   Complete the table to show the specific information given in the example.

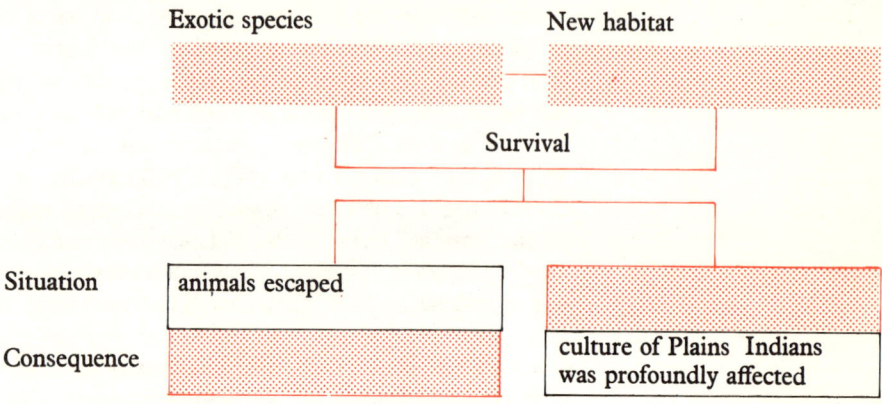

3   Why did the exotic species survive?

Activity 6

Each of the following pairs of statements contains a prediction and the circumstances on which the prediction is based.

1   Identify the circumstances and prediction in each pair.

a   Populations increase ......   the provision of adequate diets becomes urgent.

b   Traditional methods of food production are insufficient ......   new ones have to be found.

c   It is necessary to use food substitutes ......   there is not enough conventional food.

d   Fossil fuels run out ......   they are used at their present rate.

e   Fossil fuels are exhausted ......   alternative sources of energy are found.

f   There is a fuel shortage ......   solar energy is developed.

Part 5   APPLICATION OF READING STRATEGIES TO A PASSAGE CONCERNED WITH HYPOTHESES

2   Write each pair of statements in a complete sentence.

Example:
Everyone will live in cities in 2023......   the present rate of urbanization continues.

(Prediction)   (Circumstances)

Everyone will live in cities in 2023 if the present rate of urbanization continues.

**Part 5
Application of reading strategies**

We are now going to study a passage which shows how hypotheses are used in investigation. The passage also shows the role of the concepts studied in other units (definition, classification, etc.) in investigation.

AN INVESTIGATION INTO STUDENT PERSONALITY AND ACADEMIC ATTAINMENT

The Problem
The starting-point of this project was the realization that many students in universities either fail their courses or do not achieve their full potential. In some universities failure rates are alarming for both students and staff. Apart from those students who fail, lack of achievement is often evidenced by those who change from one course to another or show signs of boredom. There could be many reasons for these phenomena but it occurred to us that two questions were particularly relevant. Are students accepted for courses which are most suitable for them? How can they be helped to overcome their academic problems? By narrowing these questions down and interpreting them from a psychological point of view, a research design emerged. It was decided to investigate the characteristics of students entering universities and relate these to their academic success.

1   Complete the table to show the structure of information in the passage.

Unit 6 HYPOTHESES

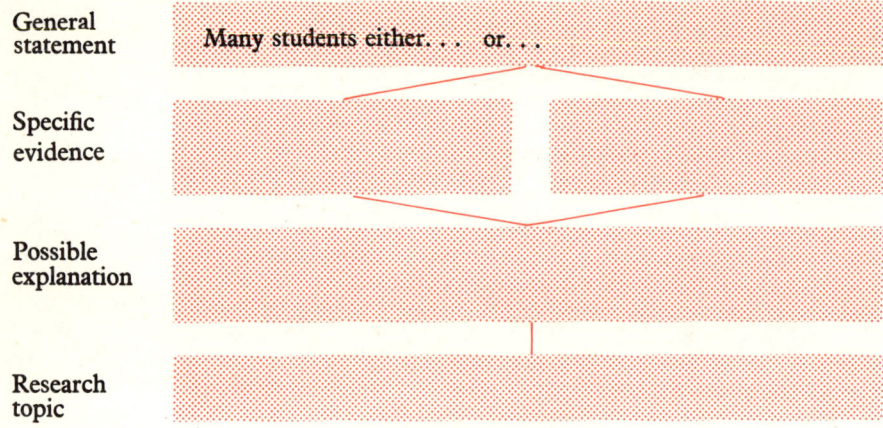

General statement: Many students either... or...

Specific evidence

Possible explanation

Research topic

2   What was the purpose of making the possible explanation more specific?

A review of the literature indicated which characteristics were likely to be relevant to academic success. It was decided that the most important variables would be motivation, study habits, personality and the students' reactions to the physical environment in the institution. We were particularly interested in the students' personality. As a way of distinguishing the range of factors that this term covers, we decided to adopt a working definition of personality. Amongst numerous definitions we found the following by Allport (1963) which referred to 'the dynamic organization within the individual of those psychophysical systems that determine his characteristic behaviour and thought'. If this definition is accepted, it appears inevitable that personality will be an important factor in academic success. The measurement of personality is, however, far from simple. Eysenck hypothesized two important yet distinct dimensions underlying human behaviour: extroversion and neuroticism. On one dimension we can describe people as neurotic or stable. On the other dimension, people range from extroverts to introverts. Neuroticism is characterized by unnecessary worrying and by general nervousness. The stable person, on the other hand, shows behaviour which is generally controlled; he tends to be

Part 5 APPLICATION OF READING STRATEGIES TO A PASSAGE CONCERNED WITH HYPOTHESES

reliable, and calm. The typical extrovert is sociable, likes parties, has many friends, needs to have people to talk to and does not like studying by himself. He enjoys excitement, takes chances and quick decisions. We may therefore define an extrovert personality as one whose interests are mainly directed outwards to the external environment rather than inwards to the thoughts and feelings of the self. The typical introvert, on the other hand, is a quiet sort of person who likes books rather than people. He does not make friends easily and tends to plan things carefully in advance. It is useful to identify individuals with above and below average scores on each characteristic and to describe four personality 'types'—stable extroverts, stable introverts, unstable extroverts and unstable introverts.

3   What is the purpose for this investigation of defining personality?
4   Why is personality important for academic success?
5   What bases for measuring personality are mentioned?
6   Based on the definition of the extrovert personality write a definition of the introvert personality.
7   Complete the table to show the differences between extroverts and introverts.

General		quiet
Attitude to people	has many friends	
Attitude to study		
Decision-making		

The hypotheses
Early research in the area indicated that in general neurotic introverts seem to make the most success-

ful students. More recent research, however, has altered the picture. Introversion is consistently related to good degree results but the effect of neuroticism is far from clear. It has seemed to be dependent on area of study. Thus in a previous study in this university it was found that students of psychology tended to have a high degree of neuroticism, while students of engineering appeared in general to be stable. We therefore formulated two main hypotheses:

1   Introverts succeed more frequently than extroverts in all areas of study.

2   Success in arts subjects is associated with neuroticism while success in science subjects is dependent on stability. One would expect, therefore, that students with good examination results would have above average scores on the appropriate characteristics and that students who failed would show opposite personality features.

8   What is, according to the previous research, the relation between:
    a   neuroticism and academic success
    b   introversion and academic success?

9   On what evidence are the two hypotheses based?

10   What deductions were made from the hypotheses?

The sample

In selecting the sample it was decided to take into account the following considerations:

1   Universities can be grouped acccording to status (whether they are private or state), size, geographical location and predominant faculty or special areas of interest. Some universities have a technological emphasis, for example; others have a faculty of particular importance, such as medicine or engineering.

2   Students can be classed according to age, sex, field of study, etc. We divided field of study very broadly into arts subjects (languages and social sciences) and sciences (pure and applied). We also took into account the home background and present

place of residence so that we considered separately those who live at home while studying and those who do not live with their family. The latter group can be subdivided into those who live in student hostels and those who live in private houses.

An attempt was made to obtain a sample which was as representative as possible of a wide range of students and institutions.

11   Use the following information about four different universities to group them according to the criteria mentioned in the paragraph.

University A. State. Situated in the capital. 15 000 students. Facilities for the study of most subjects.

University B. Situated in the capital. Private. 4000 students. Arts and pure sciences.

University C. 12 000 students. State. In the north. Main faculty: metallurgy.

University D. 4500 students. State. Situated in the south. Main faculty: veterinary science.

12   Draw a diagram to show how students can be divided according to their place of residence.

13   What is the purpose of classifying students and universities in this investigation?

Obtaining the data
Academic attainment was measured by the degree of success in the requisite tests and examinations of the students' own faculties. We decided to use a set of published self-assessment tests of personality. Students who agreed to participate were sent postcards three days before the test and we visited each institution to administer the test. While we did this we had an opportunity to get a general impression of the institution itself. There were marked differences between those we visited. Some were modern, with pleasant well-designed buildings and trees and gardens to create a relaxed

working environment. Some had attractive well-lit lecture rooms with special facilities for seminars and students' recreation. We saw others, however, which were less attractive. One had extremely large, noisy classrooms with broken and highly uncomfortable furniture. The paint was coming off the walls and students often had great difficulty in seeing the blackboards.

The reaction of students to their surroundings was a little surprising. It was, of course, natural that there should be complaints in those institutions with very poor facilities. What was more surprising was that there proved to be an equal number of complaints in institutions with very good facilities. In some of the latter, students found their physical environment monotonous, while in others what was unpopular was the quality of the teaching itself. Strangely enough, the institutions which seemed to arouse fewest complaints were those where facilities were neither remarkably good nor remarkably bad. We therefore suggest that students are more interested in the quality of the teaching they receive than in the impressiveness of their surroundings.

14   How were academic success and personality measured?

15   Which of the following characteristics of the physical environment does the writer mention?

size of classrooms   quality of furniture
ventilation   lighting
heating   library facilities
design of the surroundings

16   Complete the table to show levels of generality:

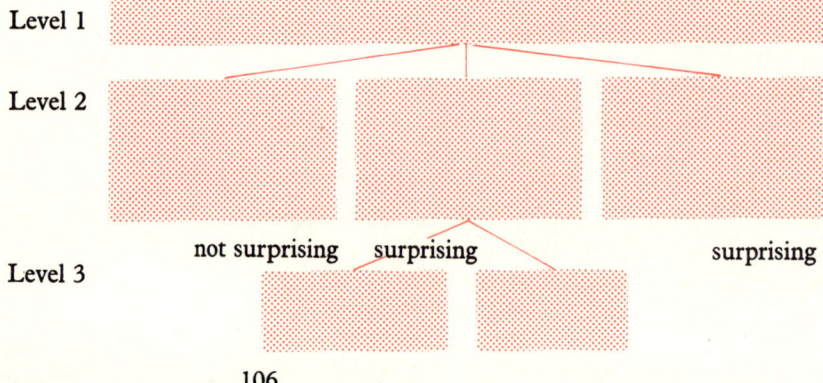

Level 1

Level 2

Level 3   not surprising   surprising   surprising

Part 5 APPLICATION OF READING STRATEGIES TO A PASSAGE CONCERNED WITH HYPOTHESES

17   What conclusion was drawn about the reaction of students?

PRELIMINARY RESULTS

We give here some extracts from our findings.

Study habits

We asked students to indicate the proportion of time they had spent on various types of studying in the previous semester and in the week preceding the tests. Arts students spent most of their time in reading recommended books and background reading, and writing essays. Pure and applied scientists, however, had spent most of their time working on set problems and writing up practicals. 22% admitted that they had spent no time at all reading recommended books during the preceding term.

18   This suggests that:
    a   Science students work less than arts students.
    b   Science students need to do more writing than arts students.
    c   Neither arts nor science students spend much of their time reading recommended books.
    d   Science students read less for their studies than arts students.

Personality

On the whole our hypotheses were substantiated. Introversion did seem to be closely related to academic success. This was particularly noticeable with mathematicians and with pure scientists generally. It was least true of students of engineering and languages, where there was practically no difference between the percentage of successful extroverts and introverts. Neuroticism, too, seemed to be a significant factor and was related to the students' own area of study. For example, applied scientists contrast with pure scientists in that the former have a much higher degree of neuroticism. Successful language students, too, have particularly high scores on the neuroticism scale. The

Unit 6   HYPOTHESES

outstanding characteristic of social scientists, on the other hand, is their emotional stability.

19   Complete the following diagrams:

GENERAL STATEMENT	introversion...
	exception supporting statement
GENERAL STATEMENT	
SUPPORTING STATEMENTS	1 3
	2 4 Social scientists are stable.

20   Based on the whole paragraph make a table showing:
    a   subject of study
    b   corresponding degree of introversion and neuroticism.

21   Refer back to the original hypotheses and decide to what extent they were substantiated.

CONCLUSION
We hope that our results, if confirmed by further research, could be taken into consideration when advising students on their choice of field of study. We would recommend that all students should be given personality tests and that they should be advised to study subjects in which they are most likely to be successful.

22   What practical application is suggested for the research:
    a   in general
    b   specifically?

Reading
and Thinking
in English

Discovering
discourse

Notes on the units

Key

Notes on the units

These notes give more detailed guidance, where required, on how to handle certain components of individual units.

Unit 1: Introductory unit

Bear in mind that the purpose of the unit is to draw students' attention to a number of reading strategies —you may wish to provide extra practice at certain points, but be careful not to 'overteach' the points.

Part 1

This part is designed to make students realize that communication consists of symbols grouped into patterns of different levels. Ask students to read up to **Activity 1** and check understanding. You may ask them to give other examples of different kinds of symbols and patterns. After students have done Activity 1, discuss their revised versions and draw their attention to the grammatical or lexical changes they made and how these differ in meaning from the original.

Activity 2 After students have read the passage silently ask them to say what is wrong with it—the two questions after the passage will then help them make their answers more precise.

Part 2

Activity 3 If students are unfamiliar with the concepts of contrast, cause-consequence, etc. introduce them before the activity by giving pairs of sentences and asking students to identify the relationship. Point out that even when using a bilingual dictionary it is still necessary to use the context to choose the appropriate meaning of a word. If you wish students to use a bilingual dictionary you may ask them to look up the words in the list—they will probably find that the context is more helpful.

Part 3

Encourage students to 'brainstorm' and suggest a variety of ideas—you should not exclude their suggestions unless they clearly show a misunderstanding of the topic. If you wish, choose a short passage, tell students its topic, ask them to predict the contents and then show them the passage for them to find how much of what they predicted is included. This will probably make them realize how predicting the contents helps a reader 'find his way' through a passage.

Part 4

Activity 8 Point out that according to the purpose they choose, students will have concentrated on different parts of the passage and read it in different ways. It is very important that students should learn not to read every word in a passage with equal attention but develop an ability to look for the part of a passage they need to read for a particular purpose and concentrate on that part. Activity 9 is designed to remind the students of the contents of the unit and to provide an introduction to the summary writing which is included in subsequent units.

Part 5

Use the picture on page 12 to introduce the topic of conformity and how people are persuaded to think or behave like others (e.g. advertisements, political propaganda etc.). Make sure that students are aware of the reading strategies they are practising at any particular time. **Purpose in reading**: it is particularly important to make sure that students read rapidly in order to answer the questions— discourage 'word by word' reading, and set a time limit which will force them to read through the passage quickly. Make sure that students answer the comprehension questions before the language study questions. Discuss answers to both types of questions, and help students to decide which answers are acceptable.

Suggested final activity. Ask students to reproduce as closely as possible the experiment described in class (it will of course be necessary to obtain genuine 'victims'). Get them to write an account of what happened—do not be surprised if the results are very different from those mentioned in the passage.

Unit 2: Generalizations

Part 1
Activity 1 You may wish to give other examples in order to make sure students understand the differences between the more general and the more specific statements, e.g. which of the following is most general and which is most specific:
a   80% of students passing French with distinction at University X are female.
b   Girls are better at languages than boys.
c   Female students of French are likely to achieve better results than male students.

Part 2
Introductory activity. Students name different forms of transport and suggest their functions. Make sure that students are aware of which questions refer to general and which to specific information.

Summary writing. It is important to point out to students that they must connect the generalizations together, using relevant information from the passage.

Part 3
Activity 2   Emphasize that the degree of generality of any statement can be determined only when we know its relation to other statements in the same context.

Activity 3
1   Point out that modifications often restrict the generality—e.g. *substances* → *poisonous substances*.
Activity 4 *Proposition* is used here to mean the idea that is expressed by a sentence.
1   The differences between the levels of generality may prove difficult here, particularly 'culture patterns change' and 'cultures have patterns'. Draw students' attention to the fact that 'cultures' is more general than 'culture patterns' as 'cultures' can include not only culture patterns but other aspects of culture ∴ when the two statements are in the same context, the statement referring to 'cultures' is more general.
3   It is important to choose the alternative which covers the most general points made in the passage (including the conclusion): i.e. the best alternative is c.
5   Let students study the diagrams and then discuss them.

Suggested supplementary group activity
Choose a topic and have each group write a generalization about it. Ask groups to exchange the generalizations they have written and then write two examples for the generalization they have been given. Then ask groups to return the papers and to judge how well the examples illustrate their generalization.

Part 5
Use the diagram to introduce the reading passage by asking students to say what it represents.
Purpose in reading. Make sure that all four pieces of information are chosen. However, it is not necessary for each student to choose all four pieces of information. Make sure also that students read the whole passage rapidly in order to find the information they selected.

Writing a summary. Discuss the level of generality of the statements before letting students write the summary.

Suggested final activity: group discussion. Get students to consider their class as a community and discuss the following questions:
1   Who are the members of the community (their age, sex, field of study etc.)?
2   What are the relationships between them (e.g. methods of communication, what some students obtain from others, effects students have on others, competition between them etc.)?
3   What outside physical factors affect the class? Ask students to take notes on the group's discussion

and to choose one student per group to give a brief oral report.

Unit 3: Descriptions

Part 1
It is not necessary to study each of the descriptions closely—the aim is to make students aware of some purposes of descriptions and the elements they contain.

Part 2
Introductory activities: ask students what they know of carbon, or e.g. what a pencil and a diamond ring have in common. To practise prediction, ask students what characteristics they would expect to find in the description of a substance.

Activity 1 The students may find it difficult to write sentences from note form. You could give one or two examples drawn from the passage before beginning the activity.

Part 3
Introductory activities: ask students what they know about coffee/ask students to describe a simple process familiar to them and identify the characteristics included. **Suggested supplementary activity:** ask each group of students to find or construct a diagram illustrating a process. Each group should give its diagram to another group, who attempt to write a description. The descriptions are then returned to the group which had selected the diagram and they judge the effectiveness of the description.

Part 4
You may wish to give students more practice in choosing the theme according to previously mentioned information either in this unit or in later units. This can be done by choosing passages similar to that in Activity 6 (not necessarily descriptions of processes) and exercises similar to Activity 7. Accounts of thematization and the grammar of information structure will be found in Quirk et al. *Grammar of Contemporary English* and Leech and Svartvik *Communicative Grammar of English*.

Part 5
Asking students to list aspects they will expect to find in the description of a primitive community should serve to motivate the students to the text—you may wish to ask students to discuss briefly one or more of the aspects they mention, drawing on their own knowledge of primitive communities. The vocabulary in the passage is quite rich—you should choose the vocabulary you wish students to concentrate on and not expect them to understand precisely vocabulary which is not central to the passage. Draw students' attention to the fact that the comprehension questions are concerned to develop their ability to recognize the characteristics that are included in the description (e.g. 1 and 5), to reorganize the specific information given (e.g. 2, 6, 7 and 10) and to summarize information (e.g. 4 and 8).

Suggested final activity: group discussion.

Men and Women in Modern Society
The passage on the Noanamá describes the different roles of men and women in a primitive society. Ask students to consider in groups the roles of men and women in their own society. Ask them to list, for example:
a   activities which are traditionally performed by men only or women only
b   ways in which the roles are changing.
Ask them to decide to what extent the roles of women should be different from those of men in modern society. Ask students to take notes on the group discussion and choose one student per group to give a brief oral report.

Unit 4: Definitions

Part 1
Note that the word 'masticometer' is invented—the device, however, actually exists. Make sure that students understand that a definition gives the essential characteristics of a concept—you could reinforce this with other examples including, if appropriate, inadequate definitions (e.g. PUPIL: What are Kangaroos? TEACHER: They are large, have brown hair and live in Australia. PUPIL: Oh yes, I know, my sister married one.).

Activity 1 Do not practise the difference between definitions and generalizations further at this stage as it is continued in Activity 6.

Part 2
When teaching real and nominal definitions, the important point is of the order in the sentence of the elements of the definition and how this may be determined contextually (as shown by Activity 4). It is not necessary to emphasize the conceptual difference between them. If supplementary exercises are required, get students to transform real into nominal definitions and vice versa.
Suggested group exercise: ask each group to write three definitions with the concept being defined missing: e.g. A – is a device for generating electricity in an automobile engine. The groups then exchange definitions and attempt to supply the missing concept. The answers are returned to the original groups who judge their correctness.

Part 3
Notice that transforming a definition into a generalization involves understanding the relation between the relative or participial clause and its antecedent. A useful supplementary exercise, which involves writing relative or participial clauses, would be to get students to transform generalizations into definitions. E.g.: A numismatist studies coins. → A numismatist is a person who studies coins.

Part 4
If supplementary practice is desired this can be done in the form of a guided composition. Choose a topic (e.g. microscopes) and a type of paragraph structure:
e.g. Definition-Generalization—Example. Description of types—Analogy.

Ask students to write a paragraph in groups. Help them with the relevant information as necessary. Other suitable topics would be 'The Atmosphere', 'Inflation' etc.

Part 5
Comprehension Question 5 is designed to show the importance of precise but comprehensive definitions of concepts. Emphasize this by comparing the traditional and the writer's definitions of systems. Question 8 is designed to draw attention to another example of a paragraph built around a definition. This is reinforced in the summary writing.

Suggested final activity: group discussion.
Get students to consider their institution as a system. Ask them in groups to make a brief summary of its purpose, content (components), and processes. Ask students either to write up the summary or to choose one student per group to give a brief oral report.

Unit 5: Classifications

Part 1
Make sure that students realize that classifications are based on a systematic consideration of similarities and differences. The resulting organization into groups and sub-groups can be conveniently expressed in a tree diagram like that at the end of this part.

Part 2
Activity 3 You may wish to give students additional writing practice in the two types of classification. This can be done based on tree

diagrams (you could use the diagram at the end of Part 1 or similar ones related to the students' own fields of study) or on information the students give themselves, e.g. Methods of Transportation and Communication.

Get students in groups to:
a Make a list of different methods.
b Suggest different criteria which could be used for classifying them.
c Choose one criterion and group the methods accordingly in the form of a tree diagram.
d Write a paragraph based on their diagram.

Alternatively, after stage c groups exchange diagrams and then write the paragraph. Each group then judges the effectiveness of the paragraph written about its own diagram.

Part 3
Activity 5   If additional practice is required, sentences like those in the activity can be given without the criteria in parentheses.

Part 4
Additional practice can be given as a guided composition using a procedure similar to that outlined in Part 4 of Unit 4. The paragraph structure could be, for example:

Identification—definition of—examples—comparaof classes   classes   tive description

Part 5
Suggested final activity: group discussion.
Ask groups to choose either 'punishment in the home' or 'punishment in society'. Ask them to:
a List examples of undesirable behaviour and arrange them from 'moderately undesirable' to 'extremely undesirable'.
b Say which form of punishment is appropriate for each kind of behaviour. Alternatively, if the students are particularly interested in psychology or education you could ask them to discuss a topic related to the final paragraph.

Unit 6: Hypotheses

Part 1
Make sure students have understood the situation and the evidence before they answer the questions on the hypotheses (these are best answered in groups). Discuss the answers before proceeding to the questions on the investigation. After discussing the answers to these, ask students to try and solve the mystery individually. Discuss their conclusions and the evidence for them. Show how the detective story illustrates the stages of the process outlined at the end of this part.

Part 2
Introduce the idea of hypotheses and evidence e.g. ask what evidence there is for the hypothesis that cigarette smoking causes cancer.

Part 3
Remind students that hypotheses can serve as the basis for deduction and are therefore used when designing experiments or solving problems.

Activity 2   Make sure that, even if students see the answer to the problem quickly, they answer the six questions on the problem.

Part 4
You may wish to give more practice in clauses of condition and circumstances.

Part 5
It is most important that students are aware that this final reading passage is designed to demonstrate

the relevance of concepts studied in Units 2–6 to academic investigation and also to provide some revision of concepts studied. This part, unlike the application stage of previous units, does not contain questions relating to reading strategies (reading with prediction, purpose in reading, language study questions). It is intended that students should now tackle a passage without this guidance. You could ask them to suggest a purpose for reading it and to suggest how to predict what they will find in it. It is hoped that if students have difficulties with the language in the passage they will now be able to adopt strategies for overcoming them. You could if you wish ask students to mark words or parts of the passage they do not understand and then discuss how to work out the meaning.

Suggested final activity: ask students to work in groups and plan a small investigation, e.g. students' leisure habits or methods of study. Get each group to:
define the topic of their investigation; formulate one or two hypotheses; choose and describe a sample; design a questionnaire or similar way of obtaining information; administer the questionnaire with a small number of students; analyse and discuss the results.

Key

Unit 1
Part 1
Activity 1
(Examples of changes in vocabulary and grammar are printed in italics.)

ORIGINAL	CORRECTION
1 It was pointed at the top.	The spaceship was *cylindrical*.
2 The craft was supported by three legs.	It was supported by *four legs*.
3 The legs were taller than the main body of the ship.	*The main body of the ship was taller than the legs.* / The legs were *shorter* than the body.
4 I saw a small green man with two horns.	I saw a small *red* man with *one horn*.
5 He had probably jumped from the ship as there was no ladder.	*It was not necessary for him to jump from the ship as there was a ladder.*
6 It showed a triangle surrounded by a circle.	It showed a triangle *surrounding* a circle.

Activity 2
The passage is not logical. In other words, there is no logical relationship between the ideas in it.
1 No. The words 'for example' and 'another example' are used to connect examples to a generalization, but in this passage the examples do not support the generalization because there is no relationship between them.
2 No. 'Whereas' is used to connect two contrasting ideas but there is no contrast here between 'girls learn mathematics quickly' and 'boys learn mathematics equally quickly'.
The following textual connectors should be underlined: *for example, another example, in conclusion, whereas*.

Part 2
An adze is a kind of *instrument* or *tool*. It can be used for *cutting wood*, ∴ it is similar to *a knife/an axe*. The drawing should show an instrument capable of making a tree trunk hollow.

Activity 3

dodge We can deduce that:
it is a simple photographic operation
it involves control of the contrast of different parts of a negative
there are several types of dodging including burning in and holding back.
We can deduce this by using the following relations:
general/specific: (for example, the words 'such as' tell us that a 'photographic operation' is a general term for the specific terms 'dodging' and 'masking')
method/purpose: the words 'is achieved by' tell us that dodging is a method of achieving control of contrast.

burn in We can deduce that:
it is a type of dodging
it involves the darkening of light areas
it involves the use of a piece of cardboard with a hole in it.
The following relations between 'burn in' and the context help us:
general/specific: one type of dodging is known as burning in
equivalence: burning in, the darkening of light areas
purpose/method: it is done by using a hole in a piece of cardboard.

hold back We can deduce that:
it is a type of dodging (because it involves control of contrast)
it involves making parts of the negative lighter (it is in fact the reverse process of burning in).
The following relation in the context helps us:
cause/consequence: some parts may have to be held back <u>because</u> they are too dark.

Key UNIT 1

crop We can deduce that cropping is different from printing the complete negative. Therefore it is probably printing merely part of a negative. The relation which helps us is contrast (expressed by the words 'on the other hand').

Part 3

Activity 4
1 We can predict that the passage may mention different kinds of sports. It may also describe how sports and international relations affect each other. It may mention, for example, specific occasions when bad international relations had a harmful effect on sport or vice versa. It may conclude that the relationship is good or bad or suggest how it can be improved.
2 The passage may show how important and widespread drug addiction is. It will probably give examples of bad effects of drug addiction on individuals and society.
3 The passage will probably give the names of the pieces, describe the board on which chess is played, show where the pieces are placed at the beginning of the game, list the moves which can be made and say how the game can be finished.

Activity 5
We would expect that the passage would include the following:
NAMES OF THINGS: water; clouds, mountains, sea, land, sky.
ACTIONS: fall, rise, move, evaporate, condense, precipitate.

Activity 6
We would expect to find the following:
1 A list of the reasons for the collapse of the bridge.
2 An example based on a particular country, perhaps mentioning particular alcoholic drinks and giving comparative figures for past and present consumption.
3 Women earn more at the bottom or in the middle of the profession.
4 Information about the social organization of termites.

Part 4

Activity 7
1 These are entries from a telephone directory, so a reader is probably looking for a person's telephone number or address.
2 This is a personal advertisement. The reader might be reading it for interest or he might want to meet a person of the opposite sex.
3 This is from a recipe. Probably the reader will be trying to cook a particular dish.
4 This is another advertisement. The reader may wish to buy a suitable tape recorder.

Activity 8
1 a arch and suspension bridges
   b stone, brick, wood, iron, steel, reinforced concrete
   c 1932
   d The Golden Gate bridge is the longest mentioned.
   e Primitive bridges were usually of the arch form, made of stone, brick or wood. Modern bridges may be of different types, and use iron, steel or reinforced concrete.
   f Suspension bridges are appropriate for long spans.

2 You should have underlined the parts of the text which give the above information.

3 Questions c, d and f involve finding one specific piece of information.
Questions a, b, e involve making a list of specific pieces of information.
Question e involves deduction from specific pieces of information because the reader has to notice

117

characteristics of modern and primitive bridges which are different.
Question d also requires the reader to consider several pieces of information before reaching his conclusion.

Part 5

1   Reading with prediction. The 4th and 6th statements are unlikely to be found in the passage as they are of no importance to this experiment.
2   Purpose in Reading. All the likely pieces of information are given in the passage.

a   Yes. If the group was unanimous more than half the victims changed their opinion. If the group was not unanimous, a much smaller number of people changed their mind.
b   He finds it disturbing that many people change their minds if the group is unanimous but encouraging that few people change their minds when the group is not unanimous.

Comprehension questions
1   The experiments have demonstrated that different kinds of people will change their judgements and opinions as a result of group pressure.
2   The results are disturbing because people will agree to statements that are contrary to the evidence of their senses or that contradict their beliefs. They are even more disturbing in that highly intelligent and independent people behave in the same way.
3   The cards might look like this:

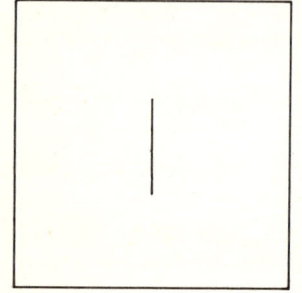
standard card
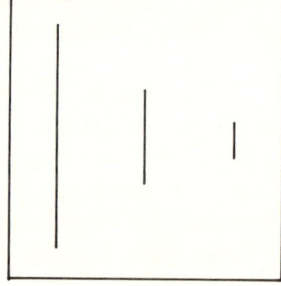

4   Most people yield to pressure when the group is unanimous. Few people yield to pressure when there is one correct judgement in the group.
5   a   The victims explained that they made the wrong choice because they thought they were suffering from an optical illusion or they were afraid to be different and consequently yielded to group pressure.
    b   The other members of the group chose the wrong line because they had been told to as part of the experiment.

Language study questions
1   'these norms' refers to 'the group's standards of behaviour and thinking'. ∴ The individual is expected to behave according to the *norms* of the group.
2   ∴ 'conform' means *to behave in accordance with the norms of the group*.
3   'this' refers to the fact that an individual is expected to conform to the standards of a group he joins.
4   Psychologists are particularly interested in the extent to which people's judgements and opinions can be changed as a result of group pressure.
5   It can be deduced from the context that 'docile' means the opposite of independent ∴ 'docile people' in this context means people who
i   *are easily influenced*.
6   The victims (that is the volunteers) are not aware of the real purpose of the experiment, ∴ they do not know its real purpose.
7   'they' refers to the other members of the group ∴ The other members of the group have been told to pick the wrong line.
8   A unanimous opinion is one that is shared by *all the members of a group*.
9   The two surprising facts are: a   more than half the victims change their opinion;
b   most of the victims know that the group choice was incorrect.
10   The effect of the pressure was that many people changed their minds, so many people yielded

Key UNIT 2

to pressure. ∴ 'yield to pressure' means 'not oppose pressure'.
11   The most encouraging finding is that few people changed their minds when there was one correct judgement in the group.

Unit 2

Part 1

Activity 1
1   Statements a, d and e do not refer to a specific time. Statements b and c refer to particular months.
2   Statements c and e do not refer to specific groups of students. The other statements refer to psychology students.
3   Statements a and e do not refer to a specific library. The other statements refer to the University library.
4   Statement b is the most specific as it refers to a specific period of time, a specific percentage of psychology students and a specific library.
5   Statement e is the most general as it refers to students and libraries in general.

Part 2
Paragraph 1
The generalization is Sentence 1: Planning of transport organization should consider the functions of transport in society.

Comprehension questions
1   The movement of people for work and leisure. The movement of goods.
2   They have little value if they are not in the right place at the right time.
3
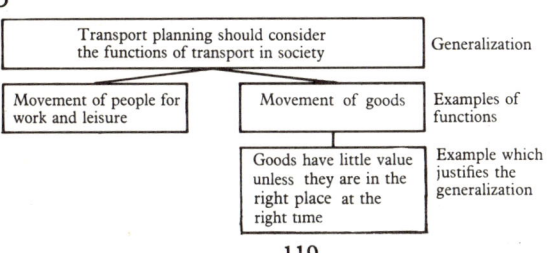

Language study question
1   c   Transport is concerned with the movement of people. It is also concerned with the movement of goods ∴ we can deduce that goods are moved by transport and are different from people. So goods are commodities such as iron, fruit, timber, etc.

Passage
Reading with prediction
All are likely except the second and the last aspects.

Purpose in reading
The 1st, 3rd and 4th aspects are all included in the passage.

Comprehension questions
4   a   Copper and some other non-ferrous ores are partially consumed (i.e. *reduced*) where they occur.
    b   Coal and iron ore are both transported to melting plants. Timber, grain, oil, meat, and wool are more valuable when they are transported to other countries.
5   It is not common for raw materials to be consumed where they occur. ∴ 'seldom' means *not commonly*.
6   The generalization is the first sentence of the paragraph.
7   The generalization is true for most of the materials mentioned in the paragraph. Here is a suggested example: Timber has to be transported because it has its full value in consumer areas.
8   The generalization is the first sentence in the paragraph.
9   Suggested example: Time is important for the transportation of fish because they must be eaten fresh.
10   Newspaper and mail depend on rapid transport. Telephone, radio and television do not.
11   Delays to car component deliveries cause *disturbance of the production lines*. This causes *massive cost increases*.
12   The generalization is the last sentence.

Key UNIT 2

13 Suggested example: Components have to be taken to the assembly plant to be used in assembling the product.
14 The transport of components; because they have to be moved at a regular rate.
15

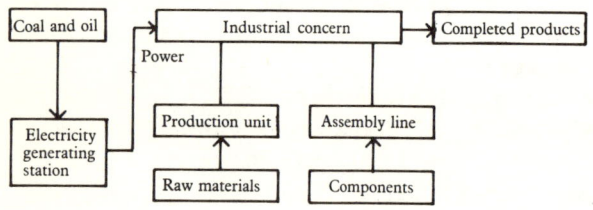

Language study questions
2 Coal and iron ore.
3 The plants are for melting ∴ iron ore is melted.
4 'Reduce' means separate the *waste* from the metal in an *ore*.
5 They are unlike in that timber has its full value in consumer areas whereas copper is often reduced at the mines.
6 The sentence in paragraph 1 is 'Goods are of little value unless they are in the right place at the right time.'
7 *held up* means 'delayed'.
8 'susceptible' means *vulnerable*.
9 'some of which' refers to some components ∴ some components must be imported.
10 c ∴ 'vital' means *extremely important*.

Summary of the whole passage
Suggested answer:
Planning of transport organization should consider the functions of transport in society. One function is the movement of goods.
 Goods have little value unless they are in the right place at the right time. Raw materials are seldom consumed where they occur in nature. Equally obvious is the importance of time in the transport of many goods.
 Transport costs are therefore a vital element in industrial productivity.

Part 3
Activity 2
Group 1 The first sentence is the generalization because the other sentences refer to specific media.
Group 2 The generalization is sentence 3 because the other sentences refer to specific types of television programmes and specific effects.
Group 3 The generalization is sentence 2 because the other sentences refer to specific products.

Activity 3
1 substances
  poisonous substances
  natural poisonous substances
  mercury
2 The most suitable title is b, because a and c are too specific.
3 a Sentence 1
  b Sentence 2
  c Sentences 3, 4 and 5
  d Sentences 1 and 2
  e Sentences 3, 4 and 5
4

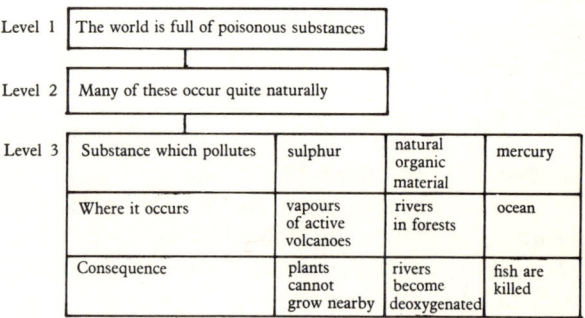

Activity 4
1 Level one: d
  Level two: c
  Level three: b and e
  Level four: a and f
  The proposition 'Culture patterns change'

assumes that cultures have definite patterns ∴ d is more general than c.
2   Sentences 3 and 4 contain more than one of the propositions.
3   Sentence c because the others do not cover the whole passage.
4   a, b and d are true in general; c and e are true in some cases.
5   The middle diagram best expresses the structure of the paragraph.

Activity 5
1   Economics students need to be able to read in English. *Most* read textbooks and *many* read journals of economics in English. Writing is much less important. *Some* write reports in English but *few* need English to write letters.
2   There is a range of purposes for which Engineering students need English. They *probably* have to read journals and they *may* attend lectures in English. It is *unlikely*, however, that they will attend seminars in English.
3   It is clear that English is necessary for the majority of students for many purposes apart from reading textbooks. They *very often* read journals in English and they *sometimes* have to read business letters. Although they *seldom* attend seminars in English, they *often* attend lectures in English.

Activity 6
There are two levels of generality in each paragraph.
1   It is probable that airline pilots will require a knowledge of English. In addition to routine business, they may have to deal with English-speaking colleagues. Although it is unlikely that they will need English to deal with emergencies, a knowledge of English for these situations is a wise safety measure.
2   Parents often find it hard to accept the idea of their children getting married. They sometimes become so attached to their children that they do not like the idea of giving them up. They sometimes need to have a child at home who depends on them so that they can feel they have a place in the world.

3   All firms need statistics. Most need to calculate the average wage of their employees. In addition, some companies need to determine statistically whether consumers like a new product.
4   Few personal assistants will be successful in their careers without a knowledge of English. Some need it for translating business letters. Most need it as well for arranging appointments with English-speaking clients.

Part 5
Questions on the diagram
1   Plants obtain food and oxygen from animals.
2   Plants depend on animals for their supply of food and oxygen.
3   Some animals hunt others, some compete for the same food, etc.
4   Some plants need shade provided by other plants. Plants may compete for light, etc.

Reading for Purpose
1   The purpose of ecology is to explain the relationships between all the different members of an ecosystem.
2   Ecologists consider man as a member of the community and consider his activities in terms of their effects on the community.
3   Animals may prey on each other and compete for the same food.
4   Plants compete for water, light, and nutrient salts.

Comprehension questions
1
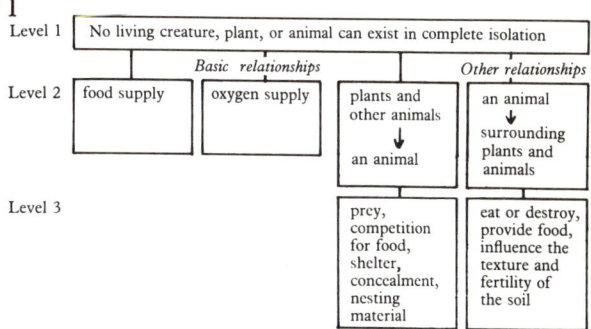

2 Dependence of plants on animals and other plants.
3 Photosynthesis; building-up of their substance; pollination.
4 The sentence concerns relationships in plant communities; therefore answer c is too limited, b is irrelevant. The correct answer is therefore a.
5 Physical factors (e.g. light, temperature, humidity). Interrelationships between living creatures.
6 Populations of different competing species exist in a state of delicate balance.
7 Each living thing fits into the whole community and has particular relationships with the other members.
8 c, because one can scarcely hope to attain it but it is well worth pursuing.

Language study questions
1 It refers to animals in general.
2 They all refer to an animal.
3 Food supply and oxygen supply.
4 Both refer to plants and animals.
5 'This dependence' refers to the relationships in general.
6 *This process* refers to photosynthesis.
7 The breaking down of organic matter in the soil by fungi and bacteria.
8–9 c Both express *addition*.
10 c The sentence *summarizes the previous paragraph*.
11 They are examples of a well-defined community.
12 *Swayed* means that the balance is moved or changed.
13 For the ecologist, the pieces of the jigsaw puzzle are the reaction and behaviour of any plant or animal. The puzzle is the whole community.
14 'It' refers to 'a piece' because the ecologists must fit each piece into the picture of the whole community.
15 Man is seen as a *piece in a jigsaw puzzle*. His activities *are seen* in terms of their effects.
16 An ecosystem consists of the whole complex of plants and animals together with the interacting physical factors of the environment.
17 The final aim of ecology is the complete understanding of ecosystems.

Writing a summary
Level 1   c
Level 2   e
Level 3   b and d
Level 4   a and f

Suggested summary
Living creatures cannot exist in complete isolation. Other plants and animals form part of the environment of every living organism. For example, animals depend on plants and other animals in many ways. Similarly, plants depend on other plants and on animals. Plants need animal respiration for the manufacture of food. In addition, animals depend on plants for their food supply.

Unit 3

Part 1
1 Suggested purposes:
a to warn; b, d, e to give information; c to persuade; f to obtain information/co-operation.

2 a, b and f describe living things (plants, animals, people); d describes substances; c and e describe objects.

3 a could be from a book or a notice; b is probably a zoo notice; c is an advertisement; d is from a book; e is a museum notice; f is a police notice.

4 dimensions: f; behaviour: b, d; colour: a, f; physical properties: c, d.

Part 2
1 a The proportion of carbon in the earth's crust is 0·19%.
  b Most diamonds are found in South Africa

Key UNIT 3

in kimberlite rock in the craters of extinct volcanoes.

Comprehension Questions
1

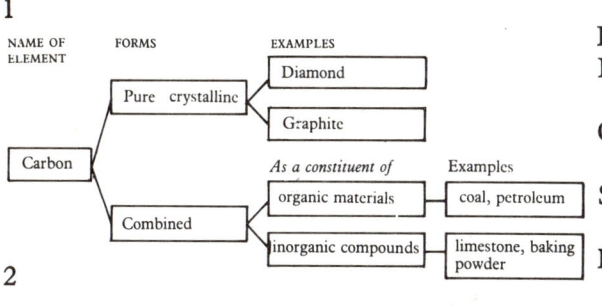

2

SUBSTANCE	MOLECULAR STRUCTURE	PROPERTY
diamonds	atoms are tightly bound	hard
graphite	Atoms are hexagonally arranged in parallel sheets. The sheets are loosely bound together.	soft slippery

∴ These properties depend on *the molecular structure (the arrangement of the atoms)*.

3   Diamonds and graphite are different in use and in electrical conductivity. They are similar in that both have high melting and boiling points.
4   Index of refraction and dispersive power are the optical properties of diamonds mentioned.
5   The best title for the paragraph is c because neither a nor b cover all the aspects described in the paragraph.
6   The title for the paragraph could be: 'Chemical reactions and properties of carbon'.
7

FORM OF CARBON	AMOUNT OF OXYGEN	RESULT
any form	large quantity	carbon monoxide
elementary carbon	excess quantity	carbon dioxide

8   Carbon monoxide is produced:
a   when any form of carbon is combined with a large quantity of oxygen at elevated temperatures;
b   in the incomplete combustion of petroleum products.

Examples of features found in the passage
Forms: There are two forms of carbon: *diamond and graphite*.
Occurrence: Diamonds are found in *kimberlite rock in the craters of extinct volcanoes*.
Structure: In graphite, atoms are arranged *in parallel sheets*.
Properties: Diamond is a *non-conductor* whereas graphite is *a conductor*.
Reactions: At elevated temperatures carbon combines with *a large quantity of oxygen* to form *carbon monoxide*.
Uses: Diamonds can be used for *jewelry and industrial tools* while graphite is used as *a lubricant and in writing instruments*.

Language study questions
1   Diamond and graphite are the two pure forms of carbon ∴ 'as' in this context means a 'in the form of'.
2   The word 'including' indicates that coal and petroleum are specific terms corresponding to the general term 'organic materials' ∴ the correct answer is c.
3   The two elementary (pure) forms of carbon are diamond and graphite.
4   Diagram a represents the structure of diamond. Diagram b represents the structure of graphite.
5   'Hard' is the opposite of *soft*. *Loose* is the opposite of 'tight'.
6   The word 'that' refers to 'the sheet': 'that above' = the sheet above; 'that below' = the sheet below.
7   They are explained by the fact that the sheets are loosely bound.
8   The word 'therefore' tells us that this ability is explained by the high index of refraction.

Key UNIT 3

9   The phrase 'the light is broken up into the colours of the spectrum' explains the meaning of 'dispersive power'.
10 'yield' in this context means 'provide' or 'produce'.
11 Artificial diamonds have been produced by heating and compressing either carbon in the form of graphite, or carbon-containing compounds such as carbohydrates. ∴ The correct answer is b.
12 'to be inert' is the opposite of 'react' ∴ it means 'does not react'.
13 Carbon monoxide is found in an automobile exhaust.
14 The words 'such as' tell us that wood, petroleum products and paper are examples of materials which burn at relatively low temperatures.
15 'This reason' refers to the fact that materials which burn at low temperatures do not continue to burn in the presence of CO_2.
16 'Carbon undergoes oxidation' means that b *carbon suffers oxidation*.

Activity 1
A suggested paragraph would be:

Silicon is always found in the combined form as silicates and silicon dioxide. Silicon is contained in most rocks. It has a diamond-like crystal structure which makes it hard and brittle. It is attacked by halogens and by oxygen when heated and it is used for the manufacture of chemically resistant steel.

Part 3
Coffee is processed where it is produced. It is roasted in industrial roasters.

Comprehension questions
1   i pulping, ii fermentation, iii washing, iv drying.
2   a gathering, drying by exposure to the sun
    b pulping, drying by hot air, freeing seeds from their coverings.
3   The dry process needs more time and equipment.
4   Pulping, fermentation and washing.
5

increase of temperature	causes →	releasing of steam etc.	causes →	changes loss of weight
		internal pressure of gas	causes →	expansion of the volume of the seeds
		chemical transformations	cause →	aroma of coffee

6   Changes in colour and texture take place during roasting.
7   Roasting is important because it gives coffee its characteristic aroma and taste.

Language study questions
1   The purpose of the processing is to separate the coffee seeds from their covering and from the pulp.
2   'pulp' in this context means *to separate* the pulp from the seeds.
3   The parts of the seeds are given the same exposure so that the parts are equally dry ∴ the correct answer is c *equally balanced*.
4   The characteristic aroma and taste of coffee appear during roasting.
5   'this' refers to the progressive raising in temperature ∴ steam is released when the temperature is raised to 200–230°C.
6   'on leaving' means 'after leaving' ∴ cooling takes place after roasting.
7   Seeds which are too light or too dark are eliminated. These are seeds which roasted badly ∴ bad roasting can cause seeds to be too light or too dark.

Activity 2
1   Series of activities or stages of the process.
2   The sequence in which two activities are performed.
3   Alternative methods of performing an activity.
4   The changes which take place in one of the stages.

5   Equipment and components used in the process.
6   The purpose of one stage of the process.

Part 4

Activity 3

The themes are:
1 Paper
2 The dry pulp sheets
3 Various materials
4 The damp layers of pulp
5 The thin sheet

Activity 4

Paragraph 1

The themes are: <u>Milk</u> is first received . . .; <u>It</u> (milk) is graded . . .; <u>The milk</u> is weighed . . .; <u>A sample of the milk</u> . . .

Paragraph 2

<u>The milk</u> then flows . . .; <u>The clarified milk</u> may then be . . .; <u>The homogenized milk</u> . . .; <u>The pasteurized milk</u> . . .; <u>The cooled milk</u> . . .

1

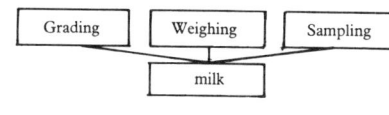

2

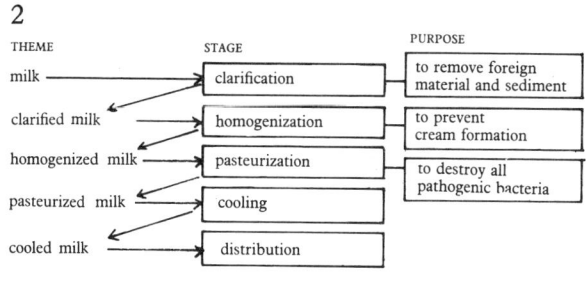

Activity 5

Suggested title: The production of protein from paraffin.

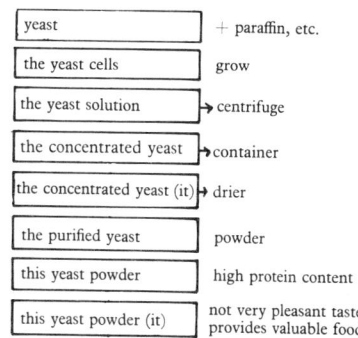

Activity 6

<u>The milk</u> goes first (to a clarifier.) (The clarifier) is a machine for applying centrifugal force. <u>It</u> consists of a rapidly revolving bowl containing (several discs.) <u>The discs</u> separate the milk into (thin streams.) <u>The streams of milk</u> then pass into (a preheater.) <u>The preheater</u> elevates the temperature of the milk to 130°F and then allows the milk to flow to (the homogenizer.) (The homogenizer) is a pump which is capable of exerting considerable pressure on the milk, thus forcing it through (a restricted opening.) <u>The small size of the opening</u> causes the milk to travel at (high velocity.) <u>This</u> causes a reduction in the size of the butterfat globules. <u>The homogenizer</u> thus prevents cream formation even after long standing.

Activity 7

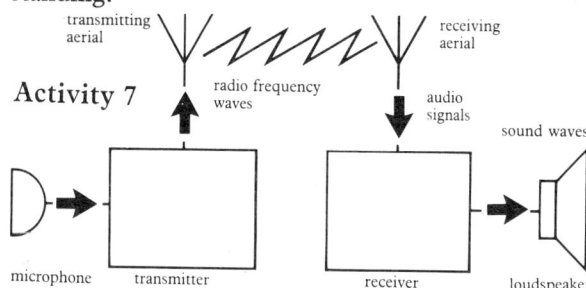

The first element in radio communication is a radio transmitter which *generates radio-frequency waves. The waves are radiated* into space by a *transmitting aerial. A portion of the radiated waves is intercepted* by a *receiving aerial. The receiving aerial often consists of* a piece of wire or a loop. *The wire* conducts small electrical signals to the radio receiver. *The signals are selected and amplified* by the *radio receiver*. The radio receiver *contains a detector*. The detector *sends out audio signals*. The *audio signals* are strengthened *by an amplifier*. The *amplified audio signal is converted* by a loudspeaker into *sound waves*.

Part 5
Application of reading strategies
Suggested list of aspects: physical characteristics, origin, living conditions, activities, social organization etc.

Comprehension questions

1

		MEN	WOMEN
physical appearance		1	2
clothes	ordinary		3
	ceremonial	5	4

2 a Wealth is indicated by porcelain beads.
  b Status is indicated by the white shirt.
  c The shirt also indicates European influence.
3 a Women use a red dye on their faces, and flowers in their hair. For ceremonies they use blue dye to cover their bodies.
  b Men wear silver pendants, strings of porcelain beads and a white shirt.
4

SUGGESTED TIME AND PLACE OF ORIGIN	EVIDENCE FOR THE THEORY
Pre-Conquest civilization of San Agustin	legend
Pre-Inca Perú	pottery
Amazon basin	—
Polynesia	Appearance Water-based existence Flowers in the hair

5 Population, language, occupation, origin and location are mentioned in the paragraph.
6

Location	Western Colombia, near the Pacific Ocean. The river San Juan flows through it.
Inhabitants	The Noanamá
Climate	humid, hot
Physical features	heavy rains, swamps, forests
Economy	near Beunaventura, Colombia's major Pacific port

7 Fishing, hunting, travelling to plantations, transporting drinks, canoe making, are activities related to the river.
8 The main steps involved in making a canoe are: selecting a tree, cutting it down, floating the trunk through creeks to the river, and shaping.
9 Maize soup, fish, meat, bananas, the fruit of the chontaduro palm, chicha, wild fruits.
10 a Men alone: hunting, repairing nets, replacing arrows, fishing, playing flutes
   b Women alone: bringing fresh water, making pots, preparing meals, looking after the children, gathering maize
   c Children: swimming
   d Men and women together: sowing maize, discussing the day's events
   e Women and children: going to the distant forest plantation to collect maize, bananas and wild fruit.

11

ACTIVITY	WHEN IT TAKES PLACE
getting fresh water from the creek	as soon as it is light
women and children go to the plantation	when the sun has risen over the river
hunting	during the night
the rainy season	before January
gathering the maize	four months after each sowing

Language study questions
1 Their heavy chest and shoulders.
2 'They' refers to the Noanamá women ∴ the women use blue jagua dye.

3   Because they wear many porcelain beads.
4   A shirt is something you wear (a garment). Other examples are: trousers, coat, shoes, jacket etc.
5   It tells us that the Chocó is a region of river deltas and coastal lowlands in western Colombia.
6   'That' refers to the language. ∴ The writer is comparing the language of the Noanamá with the *language* of the Indians of the coastal lowlands.
7   The two mysteries concerning the Noanamá are:
   a where they came from,
   b when they arrived
      ∴ these are the unknown facts.
8   The writer is suggesting a possible origin ∴ the correct answer is b *their origin*.
9   'This' refers to the last explanation given ∴ the theory that their origin was in the Amazon basin is generally thought to be the case; i.e. is generally believed to be true.
10   The writer now suggests that a different theory is possible. This is in contrast to the previous explanation ∴ the correct answer is c.
11   'They' refers to the Noanamá ∴ the Noanamá were not affected by the advance of the conquistadores. The Noanamá in this respect are unlike the Indians of the highlands ∴ the Indians of the highlands were affected.
12   'Which' refers to the advance ∴ the advance resulted in the break-up of the Andean tribes of highland Indians.
13   Because they were discouraged by the forest, the heavy rains, the humid heat and the unhealthy swamps.
14   Buenaventura is Colombia's major Pacific port.
15   The recent rise of Buenaventura as a major port.
16   A creek is a small river.
17   A jar is a kind of *container suitable for keeping drinks in*.
18   'ones' refers to canoes ∴ the children have small canoes.
19   This is the first stage of canoe making.
20   Cedar is a kind of resinous wood.
21   In this context 'rise' means c 'get up'.
22   In this context 'rise' means b 'move upwards'.
23   The context tells us that hooks, lines and nets are all used for *fishing*.
24   The context tells us that the crops are sown twice a year and that the crops are gathered four months after they are sown ∴ the most probable meaning is d *plant the seeds of a crop*.

Writing a summary

Suggested answer:

The Noanamá live in the river deltas and the coastal lowlands of western Colombia, the Chocó. It is generally believed that their earlier home lay in the Amazon basin and that sometime in the past they moved westwards across the Andes and finally halted by the Pacific. They have only recently been disturbed by foreign influence because of the rise of Buenaventura as Colombia's major Pacific port. Their activities are centred on the river. They obtain their food by fishing, hunting and cultivating maize.

Unit 4

Part 1

1   It consists of an earphone and plastic tubing. Questions 2 and 3 cannot be answered from the diagram, as the information given is insufficient.
4   Its function is to measure food crushing sounds/record the sounds of food being masticated.
5   It is inserted in the ear of the experimenter.
6   It resembles a transistorized aid.
7   The hearing aid picks up the noise produced and transmits it via an appropriate circuit to a magnetic tape.

The characteristic which enables us to define a masticometer is its specialized function. ∴ the correct answer is d. Answers a, b, c, and e could be applied equally appropriately to other instruments or objects. ∴ We can define a masticometer as an instrument which *measures food crushing sounds*.

Definition of an amplifier: An amplifier is a device which makes signals bigger.

Activity 1
1
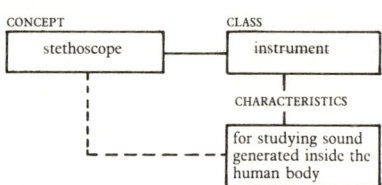

∴ 1 is a definition.

2
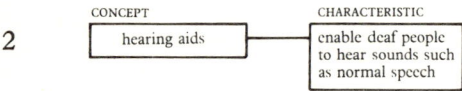

∴ 2 is a generalization.

3
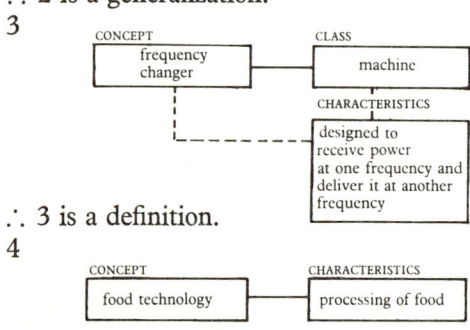

∴ 3 is a definition.

4
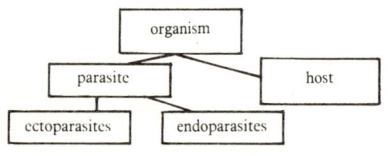

∴ 4 is a generalization.

Part 2
Activity 2
1

2 The terms defined are 'parasite', 'ectoparasites' and 'endoparasites'.

3 Ectoparasites live on the host (derive food). Endoparasites live within the host (derive shelter and protection).

4
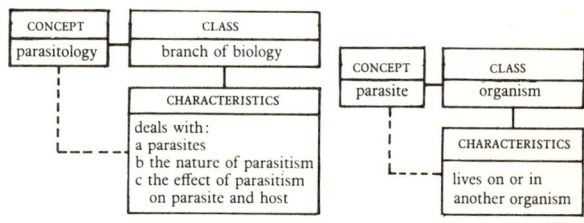

5 **Suggested answers:**

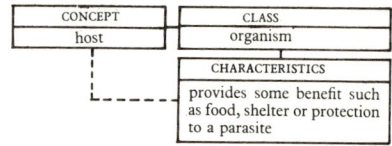

6

Organisms	living on the host	are known as	ectoparasites.
CLASS	CHARACTERISTICS		NAME OF CONCEPT

Activity 3
Kinematics is the branch of applied mathematics that deals with the motion of bodies without considering the forces which produce such motion. (Real)
Speed is defined as the rate of change of distance with time. (Real)
The speed of a body measured in a definite direction is known as its velocity. (Nominal)
Acceleration is the rate of change of velocity with time. (Real)
When the speed decreases with time the rate of decrease of speed is known as the deceleration. (Nominal)

Activity 4
– In the first definition of semantics, the new information is 'the branch of linguistics which studies

meaning'. In the second, the new information is 'semantics'. The two nominal definitions in the passage (Activity 2) are: 'Organisms living on the host are known as ectoparasites' and 'Those living within the host organism are called endoparasites'.
– The part of the passage where the theme is mentioned previously is: '. . . an organism which lives for all or part of its life on or in another organism'.

1 Cytology is the science of cell structure.
2 A person who collects coins is called a numismatist.
3 An instrument for measuring angles is called a theodolite.
4 Traditional stories which often concern the supernatural are known as myths.
5 Distillation is the process by which a liquid is evaporated and then condensed.

Part 3
Activity 5
1 Elements are chemical substances <u>that cannot be broken down into anything simpler by chemical means.</u>
2 A neutron is a particle <u>having the same mass as a proton but carrying no electrical charge.</u>
3 A trace is a substance <u>used to follow a chemical reaction or a physical process.</u>
4 Fractional distillation is the distillation process <u>in which liquid mixtures are separated into their components.</u>
5 A catalyst is a substance <u>which accelerates a chemical reaction.</u>
6 Cracking is the process <u>by which large molecules are broken down into smaller ones by means of high temperatures and pressures.</u>

Activity 6
1 A wafer is used in transistors.
2 White noise contains a wide range of adjacent random frequencies.
3 A parasitic aerial is not fed directly but gains its energy by being close to a driven aerial.
4 Automatic frequency control (AFC) controls the average radio frequency of an FM receiver.
5 A resistor introduces known resistance into a circuit.

Part 4
Activity 7
Definition: A telescope is an instrument for magnifying distant objects.

The paragraph includes **a, b, d, e**.

DEFINITION	GENERAL DESCRIPTION		DESCRIPTION OF TYPES	
A telescope is an instrument for magnifying distant objects.	objective	Collects light from the distant object and forms a real image	Refracting	Convex lens
	eyepiece	Forms a magnified image of the image	Reflecting	Curved mirror
	part	function	type	part

A *refracting telescope* is a form of *telescope* which uses a convex lens as the objective.
A reflecting telescope is a *telescope* which uses a curved mirror *as the objective*.

Activity 8
The concept defined is the biosphere.

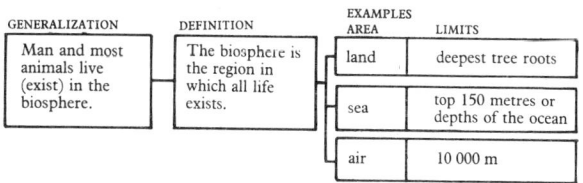

GENERALIZATION	DEFINITION	EXAMPLES AREA	LIMITS
Man and most animals live (exist) in the biosphere.	The biosphere is the region in which all life exists.	land	deepest tree roots
		sea	top 150 metres or depths of the ocean
		air	10 000 m

Activity 9
Statement 1 is a definition.
Statement 2 is a generalization.
Statement 3 is an analogy.
Statement 4 is an example.

Key UNIT 4

Comprehension questions
1 Both extend and contract under the influence of forces applied to them.
2 Increasing the price (e.g. by imposing a tax) will probably reduce demand ∴ reducing the price will probably increase demand.
3 Structure of the paragraph:

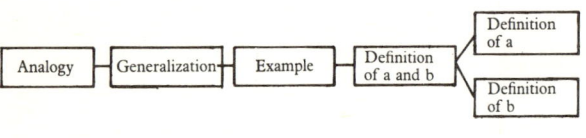

Part 5
Prediction of content

1 A factory consists of men, machines, buildings. The heart consists of auricles and ventricles. The solar system is made up of the sun, planets, and satellites.
2 Natural systems: the heart, the solar system. Man-made systems: a factory.
3 The purpose of the whole system, the relation between the components, etc.
a A group of objects united by some form of interaction or interdependence; an organic or organized whole such as the solar system or a new telegraph system.

b Systems can be defined as deliberately designed synthetic organisms comprised of interrelated and interacting components which are employed to function in an integrated fashion to attain predetermined purposes.

Comprehension questions
1 a solar system, nervous system, the brain, ecosystems.
   b telegraph system, transport systems, political and social systems,
   c hydroelectric plants, modern dairies.
2 It was realized that it was necessary to plan, design and manage a system as a whole and not the separate parts.
3 The method was new in that it developed the parts in accordance with the purpose of the whole.
4 How they interact and are integrated to achieve the purpose of the system.
5 The definition excludes natural systems since they are not deliberately designed.
6 Examples:

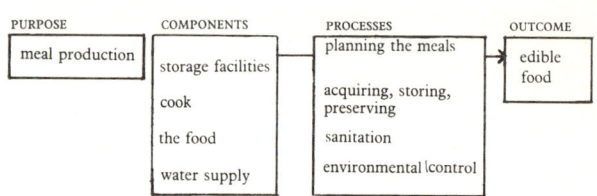

7 The definition contained in the paragraph is: A subsystem is part of a total system which is designed to carry out a purpose whose attainment is necessary in order to achieve the overall purpose of the system.

8

Concept defined	Examples of concepts	Generalization about the behaviour of subsystems	Examples of behaviour	Importance of subsystem in relation to system
Subsystem	planning, food acquisition, sanitation	Subsystems operate in an integrated fashion	Planning is integrated with and influenced by food acquisition, which then interacts with storage and preservation, preparation and the other subsystems	The effectiveness of the system depends on how well the subsystems interfunction

Language study questions
1 The brain is both a system and part of a system.
2 Because it is difficult to define precisely.
3 They realized that they could not add pieces of equipment at random.
4 The parts make up the whole ∴ the correct answer is **a** *form*.
5 The example of building combat aircraft.
6 The components interact in the performance of processes.
7 The purpose determines the components

and processes ∴ the components and processes depend on the purpose of the system.

8   A subsystem is designed to carry out a purpose.

9   *whose attainment* = the attainment of the purpose of the subsystem ∴ it is necessary to attain the purpose of the subsystems.

10   'which' refers to food acquisition ∴ Food acquisition interacts with storage, etc.

Writing a summary

Suggested answers

1   Systems can be defined as deliberately designed synthetic organisms composed of inter-related and interacting components which are employed to function in an integrated fashion to attain predetermined purposes.

2   A system consists of components, processes, a purpose and a particular outcome.

3   The content of a system is determined by the overall purpose of the system.

4   A subsystem is a part of a total system which is designed to carry out a purpose whose attainment is necessary in order to achieve the overall purpose of the system.

5   The concept of systems has application in such areas as industry, business, domestic and military planning.

Unit 5

Part 1

1 a   movement (both move)
  b   lack of movement (neither moves), production of light
  c   direction in which the roots grow (both have roots which grow downwards)

2 a   movement (B does not move)
      food (A feeds on plants, B on crude petroleum)
  b   production of noise and light (A produces noise, B emits light)
      food (C traps insects while D cultivates its food)
      production of heat and light (C produces light while D emits heat)

3 a   A and B (the roots grow downwards), C and D (the roots grow upwards).
  b   A and D both eat plants, C and D both eat insects.
  c   A and D move, B and C do not move.

4
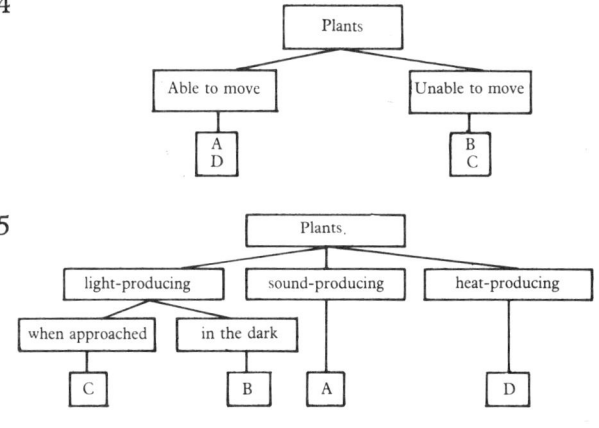

5
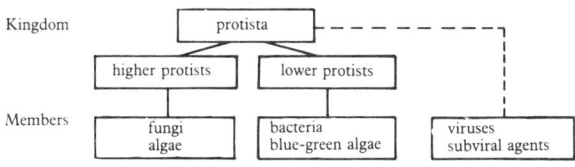

Part 2
Activity 1
Diagram 1
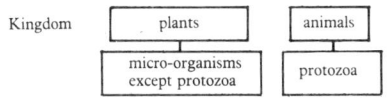

Diagram 2

1   It was arbitrary and resulted in confusions and absurdities, such as classifying viruses as plants.

Key UNIT 5

Diagram 3

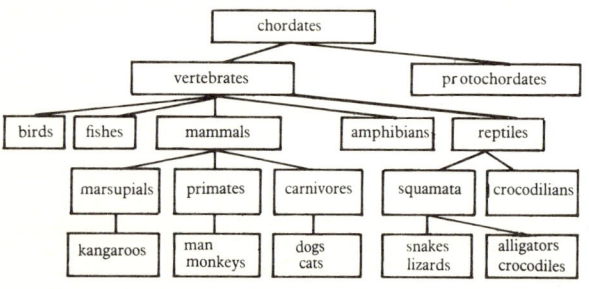

Sentences that can be underlined:

First Passage
Micro-organisms were once regarded as being members of the plant kingdom, apart from protozoa which were classed as animals.

Member: Micro-organisms
    protozoa
Class: the plant kingdom
    animals

A virus infecting an animal cannot, by any criterion, be termed a plant.

Member: A virus infecting an animal.
Class: plant.

Both these groups are placed in the kingdom protista.

Member: 'higher protists', 'lower protists'.
 Class: the kingdom protista.

Second Passage
The chordates are a large and highly diverse animal group which comprises vertebrates or animals with backbones as well as a group of animals which lack vertebrae but which resemble vertebrates in other important respects.

  Class: the chordates.
  Member: vertebrates.

The vertebrates are divided into five classes: fishes, amphibians, reptiles, birds and mammals.

  Class: vertebrates
  Member: fishes, amphibians, reptiles,
      birds, mammals.

Examples of orders are marsupials (such as kangaroos), primates (including man and the monkeys) and carnivores (including dogs and cats).

Class: marsupials Member: kangaroos
Class: primates   Member: man,
            monkeys
Class: carnivores Member: dogs, cats

Examples of these are crocodilians (including crocodiles and alligators) and squamata, examples of which are snakes and lizards.

Class: reptiles   Member: crocodilians,
           squamata
Class: crocodilians Member: crocodiles,
           alligators
Class: squamata Member: snakes,
           lizards

Examples of markers of the class-member relationship

Passage 1 be members of, be classed as, be termed, be placed in, constitute.
Passage 2 comprise, be divided into, be subdivided into, be classified into, consist of.

Activity 2
The classification belongs to type 2 (general → specific)

1 a the use to which a commodity is put

b processes involved
c for retail shops the criterion of use is appropriate.

2 The criterion of use helps us understand the reasons for consumer behaviour.
3 The criteria must be operationally reasonable—it must provide information about how decisions are made.
4 Weight.
5

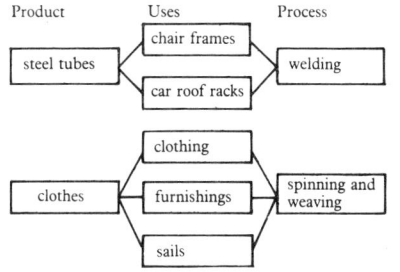

Activity 3
Examples of paragraphs

TYPE 1: Carbohydrates can be classed as energy-producing foods while proteins are termed cell-building foods. They are both organic foods. Iron, calcium and phosphorus constitute the class 'inorganic foods'. Inorganic and organic foods make up the class of food substances.

TYPE 2: Vitamins can be divided into two groups—those which are water-soluble and those which are fat-soluble. The former group consists of the vitamin B complex and vitamin C. An example of the vitamin B complex is biotin.

Part 3
Activity 4
Criteria used –
Pre-Mendeleev: properties
Mendeleev: atomic weight
Post-Mendeleev: atomic number

Basic biological criteria: anatomical, ecological and genetical facts
Other biological criteria: behaviour (e.g. feeding habits)

Markers of criteria: based on, the basis, with respect to.

Activity 5
1 Speech sounds can be classified with respect to their place in the syllable.
2 Consonants can be subdivided into groups according to their place of articulation.
3 Consonants can be classed into groups based on their manner of articulation.
4 Vowel sounds can be separated according to the part of the tongue which is raised.
5 Vowel sounds can be divided into groups based on the degree to which the tongue is raised.

Part 4
Activity 6
1 Musical instruments are classified on the basis of the principles of acoustics. Idiophones can be classified according to how they are made to vibrate. Aerophones are subdivided according to the nature of the device for interrupting the air flow. Cordophones are subdivided according to the way in which they are made to vibrate.
2

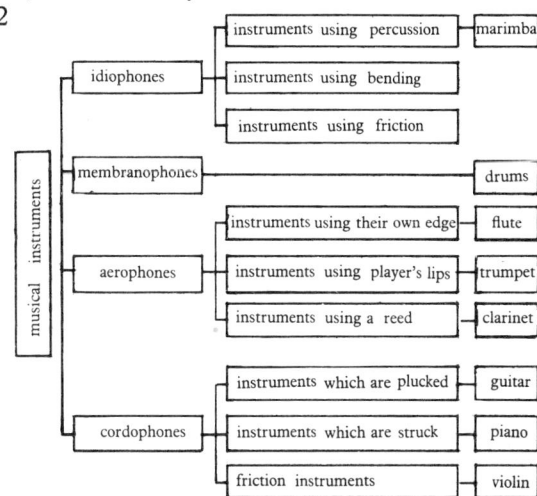

Key UNIT 5

3   The two definitions in the passage are:
Idiophones are instruments made of materials which are inherently resonant. Membranophones are instruments which produce sound by means of the vibration of a tight membrane.

We can define the other two groups in a similar way as follows:
Aerophones are instruments which consist of a body enclosing a column of air and a device for interrupting the air flow. Cordophones are instruments which emit sound by means of the vibration of a tightly-stretched string.

Activity 7

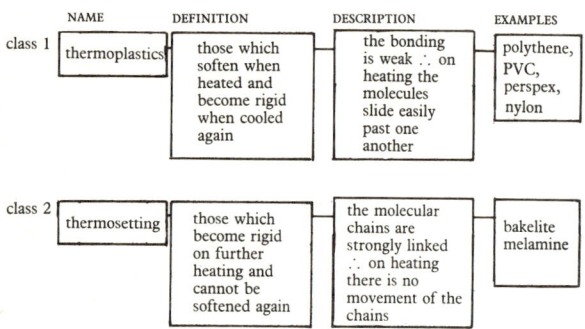

Part 5
Questions for prediction

1 a In one situation the learner is human, in the other, the learner is an animal.
   b One situation involves complex intellectual activities, the other involves a spontaneous reaction of the body.
   c In one situation the learning takes place in a library, study, or classroom; in the other it takes place in a laboratory.

2 b is true for both situations as both studying and responding in a new way involve a change in the learner.

Purpose in reading

a Any more or less permanent change of behaviour which is the result of experience.
b The Skinner Box experiments.
c The bringing up of children; the fight against crime.
d One regards all learning as forms of S-R learning. The other emphasizes cognitive organization and learning strategies.

Comprehension questions

1   Because plants can change their behaviour as a result of experience.

2   One regards 'higher mental processes' as a complex form of animal stimulus-response learning. The other regards S-R learning as being irrelevant to the process of human learning.

3   These are said to be 'extreme approaches'. It is therefore implied that there are more moderate approaches which are a compromise between the two extremes. For example, a less extreme approach would be to think that some, but not all human learning can be explained in terms of S-R associations.

4
```
                conditioning
               /            \
        classical         instrumental
           |              /          \
    use of rewards  use of punishment
                      /           \
                escape         avoidance
                training       conditioning
                               /        \
                           passive     active
```

5   The type of reinforcement used.

6   Instrumental conditioning (or operant conditioning) is an experimental procedure in which an animal is given reinforcement after it spontaneously makes a particular response, and the intensity of the response then increases.

7   In active avoidance an animal makes a specific response in order to avoid punishment. In passive

avoidance an animal must learn not to make a response which is punished.

8 The examples show that conditioning is relevant for society and education. This relevance is clear for the examples ∴ the correct answer is b.

9

LEARNING THEORY	EDUCATIONAL IMPLICATIONS
Skinnerian	programmed learning, teaching machines
non S-R theories	view of language learning as a cognitive process
Harlow's theories	Curricula which emphasize learning strategies

Language study questions

1 Between the varied set of learning activities.
2 The interaction between the learner and the environment brings about a change in the learner. It causes a change to occur ∴ the correct answer is c *cause to happen*.
3 'underestimate' means to give too little importance to something. 'It would be a mistake to give too little importance to the differences' therefore means that the differences are important.
4 'Two stimuli are paired' means that two stimuli are given together ∴ the correct answer is a *association*.
5 'Which' refers to the pairing ∴ the first stimulus elicits the response previously made by the second stimulus.
6 The Pavlovian experiment with dogs.
7 Because the response has been reinforced.
8 'The latter' refers to avoidance conditioning ∴ avoidance conditioning can be subdivided into passive and active avoidance.
9 The electric shock which is used as a form of punishment is mild ∴ the most probable meaning is d *not strong*.
10 'It' refers to punishment ∴ parents use punishment.
11 A theory can be proposed or verified. The most probable meaning is a *propose*.

12 The paragraph is concerned with the educational implications of psychological theories ∴ the most probable answer is b *based on*.

Writing a summary

Suggested answer:
Learning can be defined as any more or less permanent change of behaviour which is the result of experience. The two main approaches to learning are S-R theories and cognitive theories. The simplest type of S-R learning is conditioning which can be separated into classical and operant conditioning. The essential operation in classical conditioning is the pairing of two stimuli as a result of which the first stimulus elicits the response previously elicited by the second stimulus. In instrumental conditioning an animal is given reinforcement after it spontaneously makes a particular response, and the intensity of the response then increases. An example of a non-behaviourist theory is the 'learning to learn theory' of Harlow. This philosophy is behind many developments in present-day curricula where the emphasis is put on learning strategies.

Unit 6

Part 1

Hypothesis 1: The evidence against this is that she was able to give an accurate description of the film she was watching at the time of the crime.

Hypothesis 2: The evidence for this is that, according to Colonel Crab, there was no one in the corridor at the time Plum said he was there.

Hypothesis 3: There is no evidence to support this hypothesis. In fact, the evidence of the telephone operator contradicts it.

Hypothesis 4: No, but it suggests that it was possible that Colonel Crab committed the crime.

The investigation

If Colonel Crab's story was correct, Tony Plum was not telling the truth when he said that he did not move from the corridor. (Colonel Crab stated that there was no one sitting in the corridor at 3:55.) If Tony Plum was telling the truth, then either Colonel Crab did not go past him or Plum did not notice the Colonel (perhaps he was too busy reading). The important piece of evidence is that of the lift technician. If the lifts were not working, then Colonel Crab was lying ∴ he did not use the lifts but went up the stairs. Consequently he did not pass the place where Tony Plum was sitting. This evidence made the Inspector conclude that all the suspects were telling the truth except Colonel Crab, and that Colonel Crab had committed the murder.

Part 2

The main hypothesis about how the earth is changing is that the continents of the earth are moving apart.

1

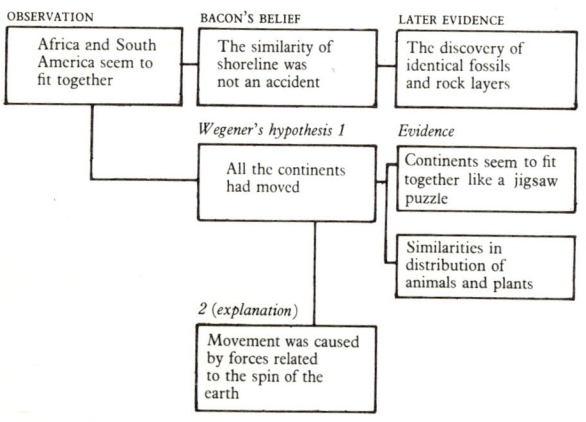

2 Oceanography has revealed a system of rifts running down the middle of all the oceans and round the continent of Antarctica. It has also shown that the rifts are opening. This evidence was obtained by methods such as drilling to obtain rock and mud samples from the ocean floor.

3 The other evidence that supports the main hypothesis is that rocks in different continents can be matched according to their pole positions. This evidence was obtained by the study of paleo-geomagnetism.

4 The left-hand drawing is the correct one.

Part 3
Activity 1
Comprehension questions

1 It is known that retardation of growth may be caused by deficiency of thyroxin or deficiency of a hormone S.

2 The biologist has to determine which type of deficiency has caused the retardation of a particular group of rats.

3 The difference between the two approaches is that the first approach consists in making good the deficiency. The second approach involves first of all causing the retardation, then bringing about a return to normal growth.

∴ the procedure that both approaches have in common is to make good the deficiency.

4

	HYPOTHESES	CONCLUSIONS
Approach 1	Giving the rats thyroxin leads to normal growth	The rats were probably deficient in thyroxin
	Giving hormone S results in normal growth	The rats were deficient in hormone S
Approach 2	Removing the thyroid glands leads to the same type of retarded growth	The rats were deficient in thyroxin
	Removing the pituitary leads to the same type of retarded growth	The rats were deficient in hormone S
	The experiment to make good the deficiency leads to normal growth	The conclusions from the results of the operation will be confirmed

Activity 2

1 The consequence will probably be that the dog will attack the sheep.

2 We can deduce that the sheep will eat the hay.
3 ∴ the farmer must take the sheep first.
4 Suggested diagram:

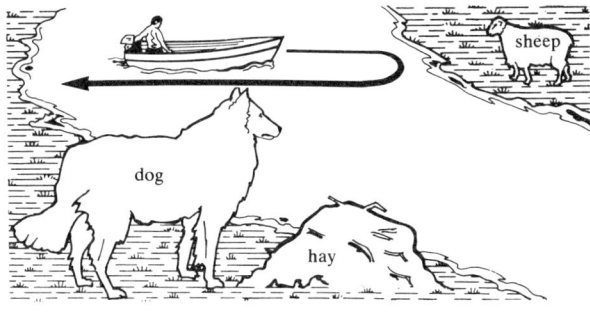

5 Hypothesis a   implies that the dog and the sheep will be left together.

   Hypothesis b   implies that the sheep and the hay will be left together.

   Hypothesis d   involves either a or b and would not therefore solve the problem.

∴ the correct answer is c (because at no time does the farmer leave the sheep and the hay or the sheep and the dog together).

6 The farmer has to cross the river seven times.

Part 4
Activity 3
1 The observer must be between the sun and the rain. The sun must not be too high.
2 It is necessary for light from the sun to be dispersed by drops of water.
3 The occurrence of a rainbow depends on the presence of drops of water in the air.

Activity 4
1 Diagram:

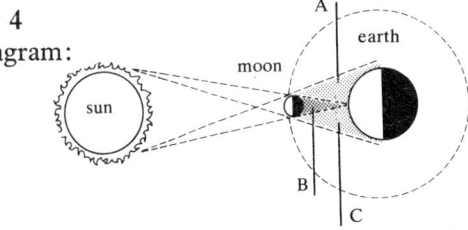

2 a There is an eclipse of the sun when the moon comes between the earth and the sun.
  b You see a total eclipse if you are in the region marked B (no light at all is received from the sun.) You see a partial eclipse if you are in regions A or C (light is received from only part of the sun.)

3 When the earth comes between the moon and the sun, light from the sun cannot reach the moon. If this happens, there is an eclipse. There will not be a total eclipse unless the moon lies in the umbra. If the moon lies in the penumbra there is no eclipse, since the moon merely becomes less bright. If the moon lies between the umbra and the penumbra, it is partially eclipsed.

Activity 5
1

	ALTERNATIVE 1	ALTERNATIVE 2	ALTERNATIVE 3
Given situation	a Food is too scarce b Food getting is too competitive c Predators are too numerous	Food is abundant and predators are absent	The balance between food and predators is just right
Predicted Consequence	The exotic species will not survive	It will rapidly multiply to plague proportions and disrupt the life of every organism in the habitat	It may produce important secondary ecological consequences

2

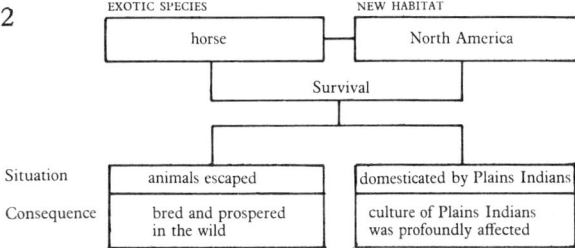

Key UNIT 6

3   The exotic species (the horse) survived because the balance between food and predators was right.

Activity 6

a	Populations increase (circumstances)	the provision of adequate diets becomes urgent (prediction)
b	Traditional methods of food production are insufficient (circumstances)	new ones have to be found (prediction)
c	It is necessary to use food substitutes (prediction)	there is not enough conventional food (circumstances)
d	Fossil fuels run out (prediction)	they are used at their present rate (circumstances)
e	Fossil fuels are exhausted (circumstances)	alternative sources of energy are found (prediction)
f	There is a fuel shortage (circumstances)	solar energy is developed (prediction)

2 a If population increases, the provision of adequate diets will become urgent.
   b If traditional methods of food production are insufficient, new ones will have to be found.
   c It will be necessary to use food substitutes if there is not enough conventional food.
   d Fossil fuels will run out if they are used at their present rate.
   e If fossil fuels are exhausted, alternative sources of energy will have to be found.
   f If there is a fuel shortage, solar energy will have to be developed.

Part 5
Comprehension Questions

1

General Statement	Many students either fail their courses or do not achieve their full potential
Specific evidence	Some failure rates are alarming for both students and staff / Some students change course or show signs of boredom
Possible explanations	1 Students are not accepted for courses which are most suitable for them 2 Students are not helped to overcome their academic problems
Research topic	The characteristics of students entering universities and their relation to academic success

2   The explanations were narrowed down in order to make them suitable as a basis for a research design.

3   Defining 'personality' helped to distinguish the range of factors that the term 'personality' covers.

4   Because according to the definition adopted, it determines an individual's characteristic behaviour and thought.

5   It is suggested that personality can be measured in terms of the individual's characteristics in two dimensions—extroversion and neuroticism.

6   The introvert personality is one whose interests are normally directed inwards to the thoughts and feelings of the self rather than outwards to the external environment.

7

	EXTROVERT	INTROVERT
General	sociable	quiet
Attitude to people	has many friends	likes books rather than people; does not make friends easily
Attitude to study	does not like studying by himself	likes books rather than people
Decision-making	takes chances and quick decisions	tends to plan things carefully in advance

8 a Research first indicated that neuroticism was associated with academic success. Later, it seemed dependent on the area of study.

b Introversion has been constantly related to academic success.

9 The hypotheses are based on the conclusions of previous research, particularly on a study in the same university which indicated that psychology students are neurotic while engineering students are stable.

10 It was deduced that students with good examination results would have above average scores on introversion and students who failed would have above average scores on extroversion. It was also deduced that successful arts students would have high scores on neuroticism, while unsuccessful arts students would not; and that successful science students would have high scores on stability, while unsuccessful ones would not.

11
ACCORDING TO STATUS	ACCORDING TO SIZE
B is private	A and C have over 10 000 students
C and D are state universities	B and D have less than 10 000 students

ACCORDING TO LOCATION	ACCORDING TO PREDOMINANT FACULTY
A and B are located in the capital	A has no predominant faculty
C and D are located in the provinces (C in the north, D in the south)	C and D each have one faculty predominant, while B has an emphasis on more than one area

12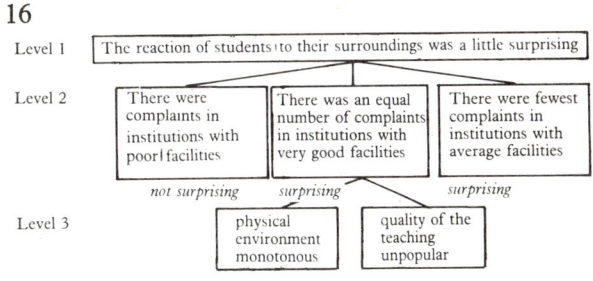

13 The purpose of classification was to obtain a representative sample.

14 Academic attainment was measured by the degree of success in the requisite tests and examinations of the students' own faculties. Personality was measured by published self-assessment tests.

15 All are mentioned except ventilation, heating and library facilities.

16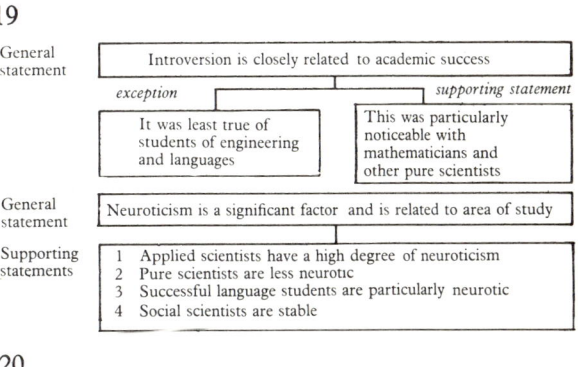

17 It was concluded that students are more interested in the quality of the teaching they receive than in the impressiveness of their surroundings.

18 c is false; a and b are not implied in the paragraph. The passage does, however, imply that reading recommended books was of little importance for the studies of science students ∴ the correct answer is d.

19
General statement: Introversion is closely related to academic success
- exception: It was least true of students of engineering and languages
- supporting statement: This was particularly noticeable with mathematicians and other pure scientists

General statement: Neuroticism is a significant factor and is related to area of study
Supporting statements:
1 Applied scientists have a high degree of neuroticism
2 Pure scientists are less neurotic
3 Successful language students are particularly neurotic
4 Social scientists are stable

20
SUBJECT OF STUDY	DEGREE OF INTROVERSION	DEGREE OF NEUROTICISM
Mathematics	+	−
pure science	+	−
engineering	+	−
languages	+	+
applied sciences	0	+
social sciences	0	−

21 The original hypotheses were:
    a Introverts succeed more frequently than extroverts in all areas of study. This was substantiated except in the case of engineering and language students.
    b Success in arts subjects is associated with neuroticism while success in science subjects is dependent on stability.
    Findings–
    Arts subjects: language students had high neuroticism but social scientists had high stability.
    Science subjects: applied scientists are more neurotic than pure scientists.
    ∴ the hypothesis was not entirely substantiated.

22   a It is suggested, in general, that the results should be taken into consideration when advising students on their choice of field of study.
    b It is specifically suggested that students should be given personality tests and advised to study subjects in which they are most likely to be successful.